THE
T. S. ELIOT
MYTH

THE
T. S. ELIOT
MYTH

ROSSELL HOPE ROBBINS

 HENRY SCHUMAN · NEW YORK

FOR

HELEN ANN

ACKNOWLEDGMENT

Permission to quote from the following books by T. S. Eliot published by Harcourt, Brace and Company is hereby acknowledged:

THE IDEA OF A CHRISTIAN SOCIETY, copyright, 1940, by T. S. Eliot. Reprinted by permission of Harcourt, Brace and Company, Inc.

NOTES TOWARDS THE DEFINITION OF CULTURE, copyright, 1949, by T. S. Eliot. Reprinted by permission of Harcourt, Brace and Company, Inc.

AFTER STRANGE GODS by T. S. Eliot, copyright, 1934, by Harcourt, Brace and Company, Inc.

POE TO VALERY, copyright, 1948, by T. S. Eliot. Reprinted by permission of Harcourt, Brace and Company, Inc.

SELECTED ESSAYS OF T. S. ELIOT, copyright, 1950, by Harcourt, Brace and Company, Inc.

MURDER IN THE CATHEDRAL by T. S. Eliot, copyright, 1935, by Harcourt, Brace and Company, Inc.

THE COCKTAIL PARTY, copyright, 1950, by T. S. Eliot. Reprinted by permission of Harcourt, Brace and Company, Inc.

THE FAMILY REUNION, copyright, 1939, by T. S. Eliot. Reprinted by permission of Harcourt, Brace and Company, Inc.

COLLECTED POEMS 1909-1935 by T. S. Eliot, copyright, 1936, by Harcourt, Brace and Company, Inc.

FOUR QUARTETS, copyright, 1943, by T. S. Eliot. Reprinted by permission of Harcourt, Brace and Company, Inc.

CONTENTS

THE

ELIOT

LEGEND

PERHAPS NO AUTHOR LIVING TODAY IS HELD IN GREATER APPAR-
ent esteem in academic circles than Thomas Stearns Eliot.
Eminent scholars and experienced critics are all but unani-
mous in their admiration. In the past twenty years few
books strongly critical of Eliot have appeared,[1] and the occasional dissenting articles are lost in journals of limited circulation,[2] leaving the legend of the greatness of Eliot virtually unchallenged. Most students of English literature are
brought up in the pattern of uncritical reverence. The recent tributes—the anthologies of Rajan (1947), March and
Tambimuttu (1948), and Unger (1948); the monographs
of Matthiessen (1935, 1947), Brooks (1939), Wilson (1948),
Gardner (1949), and Drew (1949); and the reviews of his
essays and plays in most periodicals—remain in effect indis-
criminate encomiums.

A case might be made for the judgment of Eliot as one of "the two greatest [poets] of our time." [3] But surely enthusiasm has got the better of judgment when critics extend his prestige far beyond the present age. "No other poet, except Shakespeare, has the capacity for expressing tenderness without sentimentality and without illusions." [4] Of his most recent poetical work, *Four Quartets,* one writer has stated: "Nothing greater has ever been written in the English language—that is the rather startling conclusion forced upon one, after making a serious study of this work of Eliot's." [5] Moreover, in addition to being called "the most outstanding poet," Eliot is praised as the "most influential critic" [6] in twentieth-century English literature, with "the most imposing of contemporary literary reputations." [7]

If critics who set standards in the learned reviews are so swept off their feet by the works of Eliot, it can occasion little surprise that, when the opportunity arises, the reviewers in popular magazines and newspapers show a similar exuberance. A spate of lavish praise followed the New York opening of *The Cocktail Party.* John Chapman, in the New York *Daily News,* and Robert Garland, in the New York *Journal-American,* both called it "a masterpiece." Robert Coleman, in the New York *Daily Mirror,* described it as "one of the great plays of our time."

So the adulation snowballs down from the heights of Parnassus and Kenyon into the market place; the popularizers take their cues from the deans and dons. In all quarters, Eliot is held up as the greatest modern poet, critic, and belletrist, and in many quarters as the greatest playwright. Noting the award of the Nobel prize for literature in 1948 and the Order of Merit in the same year, the man in the street is just as ready as the man on the campus to accept the dictum that Eliot is the greatest living man of letters. Consequently Eliot's influence is no longer confined to literary circles, but extends to public life.

The semigovernment agency, the British Council, lends its official approval to this prestige: "If there is anyone who, on the appropriate occasions, may speak for English letters with the voice of authority, it is Eliot. In fact there has been no one who occupied a comparable position since the reign of Samuel Johnson, The Grand Cham." [8] So it has come to pass that a writer in the less popular forms, one who has never written a best-selling novel, has become so newsworthy as to be featured on a *Time* magazine cover.[9]

Perhaps a clue to this unexpected publicizing of a poet is given by a writer in *Thought* in 1946: "But in the field of letters proper, the prestige and example of Eliot have done more than any other single factor to redirect the thought of the English speaking world toward the significance of the Judaeo-Graeco-Catholic spiritual tradition." [10] Whatever Eliot thinks, says, or does, is greeted, especially in America and in Germany (for the last few years), as the thought or action of a leader of world opinion.

Who is this Eliot who has become a virtual legend in his own time? Why is he so revered? What has he done? What does he stand for?

Eliot is generally credited with having changed the direction of British and American poetry and having advanced its techniques. Those who first came across Eliot in the years after World War I found his manipulation of poetic rhythms new and exciting. Whatever explanation of his innovations is adopted—a debt to Hopkins, a study of Anglo-Saxon practice, an interest in Langland's apparently loose prosody,[11] or the transfer into English of the metrics of the French symbolists[12]—the free-flowing lines of Eliot formed a versatile medium for the early satiric exercises, the impressive choruses of *Murder in the Cathedral,* and the conversational verse of *The Cocktail Party.* Younger poets have profited by the mobility of verse, which without apparent or sudden change can take on whatever aspect the content demands.

In addition to the fluidities of his meter, there were in the early poetry unusually clear and concrete images, an almost photographic symbolism, whose effectiveness derived from an economy of words, from personification, synecdoche, violent and disparate antithesis. It had striking lines which fixed themselves in the minds of the undergraduates of the later twenties, inciting a lasting interest in this world of terse poetry, induced by hints and fragments—"The yellow fog that rubs its back upon the window-panes"; "I have measured out my life with coffee-spoons"; "a pair of ragged claws Scuttling across the floors of silent seas." The 1917 series of *Prufrock* poems have persisted over the decades and enriched the poetic tradition.

Just as phrases from his early poems linger, so do sentences from his early prose. His criticism is flecked with quotable passages, with illuminating phrases that often sum up an involved analysis such as this line in his introduction to the anthology of Ezra Pound in 1928: "no *vers* is *libre* for the man who wants to do a good job." [13] Or where, discussing the techniques of criticism, he writes (1923): "Comparison and analysis need only the cadavers on the table; but the interpretation is always producing parts of the body from its pockets, and fixing them in place." [14] Or again, as late as 1934, in this metaphor: "The minor poet who hitches his skiff astern of the great galleon has a better chance of survival than the minor poet who chooses to paddle by himself." [15] A fresh and immediate effect is given in such characterizations as that of Donne sensing an idea "almost as if it were something he could touch and stroke." [16]

Nonacademic devotees of the Eliot cult, who sometimes lack the necessary technical erudition to assess the skills to which they give lip service, think of him chiefly as the man who has brought dignity and high seriousness to the modern stage. Among them are the reviewers who would set *The Cocktail Party,* for example, apart from other "smart" comedies because it sets the audience thinking. The *Daily Mirror* continued its review in this manner: "It is a wonderful experience in the theatre. It is a superb answer to those pessimists who say that our 'Fabulous Invalid' is on its deathbed. No theatre is expiring that gives us such mental and emotional stimulation." [17]

Yet, for all this "mental stimulation" it is remarkable how little discussion there is, in all these commentaries, of what Eliot *says* in his works. The scholars accept generally without question Eliot's favored motto: "It is never what a poem *says* that matters, but what it *is*." [18] And, while insisting that the writing seems to be significant, the popularizers admit that they cannot understand it.

This by-passing of the content is all the more noteworthy because in the past twenty years Eliot has become less concerned with the creation of "pure" literature, and more involved in the propagation of points of view. His three plays of 1935, 1939, and 1950 are definitely tendentious—and plays are the most public of all literary forms. His major critical works in prose, especially his latest *Notes towards the Definition of Culture* (1949), which received much acclaim, are sociological.

To the many people to whom Eliot is best known as a poet, his reputation continues to rest on *The Waste Land* of 1922, and not as yet so much on the poems known as *Four Quartets* (1935-1942), which are the *sole* poetry he has composed during these last two decades. Eliot, having now concentrated on criticism and cultural and social speculation, must be primarily considered a man of letters, not a poet or dramatist.

Now, without judging an author by the standards we set for a philosopher or statesman, we nevertheless have a right to hold him accountable for the meanings his words convey. Although Eliot has tended more and more to polemic and expository forms of writing, among his admirers there is what amounts to a conspiracy of silence, or at the very least a casual or purposeful disregard of the meaning in his poetry, his drama, and his prose. They ask us to accept a writer as outstanding without evaluating what he is saying to us. It is doubtful, however, whether the merits of new techniques are ever sufficient in themselves to justify a *major* reputation, unless they are accompanied by a broad and humane interpretation of life. A writer who is important only for "occupying points in the development of a major form," [19] is, Eliot himself says, not even a minor poet, but merely second-rate. On occasion, Eliot has advanced the need to go beyond evaluation by form alone as when he says: "Literary criticism should be completed by criticism from a definite ethical and theological standpoint." [20]

In any estimate of the "greatness" of Eliot, we cannot, by standards Eliot himself assents to, ignore his philosophy. "Literature—I mean again, primarily, works of imagination —has been, is, and probably always will be judged by some moral standards." [21]

Following this precept of Eliot's, let us consider Eliot's writings in the light of the opinions they express. Do they reflect a mind endowed with those powers of comprehension, grasp of essentials, insight into men's character, which we expect of a first-rate author? Let us test him by his opinions of some of the major events that have made the modern world—The French Revolution, The Civil War in America, and the Protestant Reformation.

What has Eliot to say on the French Revolution? He describes himself as "one who has never been an admirer of Republican government in France." [22] "We may deplore the French Revolution, but we must accept it as a fact." [23] Note that he speaks, not of the Reign of Terror, but of the Revolution as a whole. He has not a word to say in this statement—is it possible he does not understand?—of the destruction of feudalism and the subsequent rise and development of modern Europe which the French Revolution brought about.

> Contrast Jefferson on this same subject: in the struggle which was necessary, many guilty persons fell without the forms of trial, and with them some innocent. These I deplore as much as anybody, and shall deplore some of them to the day of my death. But I deplore them as I should have done had they fallen in battle. . . . The liberty of the whole earth was depending on the issue of the contest, and was ever such a prize won with so little innocent blood?[24]

When Pétain replaced the slogan adopted as the heritage of the Revolution with one preferred by reactionaries, Eliot sided with him, asserting: "The device Liberté, Egalité, Fraternité is only the memorial of the time of revolution: Famille, Travail, Patrie has more permanent value." [25] As often happens with Eliot, the line by itself may appear innocuous and on the surface defensible (as perhaps in some senses it might be possible to "deplore" the French Revolution). But the same sentence, in a whole corpus of similar innocent-seeming lines, turns sinister against the background of his philosophy, which in its political aspect constitutes an outspoken attack on republicanism and democracy.

This slur on the principles of the French Revolution, Liberty, Equality, Fraternity, has, as philosophic context, his support of the proto-fascist and avowedly anti-Semitic *Action Française,* voiced in two issues of his own magazine *The Criterion.* In one article (December, 1928), he praises Charles Maurras, the leader of the movement: "Most of the concepts which might have attracted me in fascism I seem already to have found, in a more digestible form, in the work of Charles Maurras. I say a more digestible form because I think they have a closer applicability to England than those of [Italian] fascism." [26] After some further comments stressing "the importance of continuity through Kingship and hereditary class," Eliot concludes: "I end by reflecting that the development of fascism in Italy may produce very interesting results in ten or twenty years. And that it is a matter of regret that England has no contemporary and indigenous school of political thought since Fabianism, and as an alternative to it." [27]

And what does Eliot have to say on the Civil War in America? He has been praising the manifesto *I'll Take my Stand* (of the so-called Southern Agrarians), characterized by Alfred Kazin in his *On Native Ground* as "the convenient symbol of an aristocratic tradition . . . in which the sense of race and community and the soil had supported a culture." [28] Eliot laments that "the influx of foreign populations has almost effaced the American 'tradition' in some parts of the North." Following these views comes Eliot's verdict: "The Civil War was certainly the greatest disaster in the whole of American history; it is just as certainly a disaster from which the country has never recovered, and perhaps never will." [29]

Here, as in his comments on the French Revolution, some historians might agree that the Civil War was "a disaster from which the country has never recovered." But would they then go along with Eliot's implications that the society based on slavery led to the "Good Life"? "The question of the Good Life is raised and how far it is possible for mankind to accept industrialization without spiritual harm. The complaint is not merely that the South was ruined and subjected by the Civil War, but that it is now well on the way towards being northernized; that coal, oil, iron and factories have altered the relation of man to his world, and that the Good and Happy Life is becoming less possible." Then comes the summation: "The old Southern society, with all its defects, vices and limitations, was still in its way a spiritual entity; and now the organization of society is wholly materialistic." [30]

As for the Reformation, in his most recent long essay, *Notes towards the Definition of Culture* (1949), it is dismissed as "the schisms of the sixteenth century . . . as the variation of doctrine, or as the disintegration of European culture." [31] Again, in another passage, an unhistorical account of the previous centuries is pointed up by his stress on the word "only." The whole of the history of Europe from 1550 to 1950 is thus belittled: "When we consider the Western World, we must recognise that the main cultural tradition has been that corresponding to the Church of Rome. Only within the last four hundred years has any other manifested itself; and anyone with a sense of centre and periphery must admit that the western tradition has been Latin, and Latin means Rome." [32]

In the case of a minor writer it would not matter so much whether his views on epochal social changes were either logical or historically true. Eliot, however, has been "enhedged with nebulous divinity," [33] and his political works have been widely translated.[34] His philosophy of life consequently must measure up to the standards of a world man of letters.

But it might be fairer to turn to what should most interest a writer—the everyday personal relations of human beings, how to bring up our children, how to get along with relatives, or with friends, or with people outside our own club or church. What has Eliot to say here?

What has Eliot to say about education? No matter how much we may find wrong with the present educational systems in England or America, there are probably very few of us who would wish to renounce our major educational advance to put the schools back under sectarian religious control and again limit education to the few. These, however, are the two main points in Eliot's program. In the *Christian News Letter,* a small sheet with a very limited circulation among Episcopalians, Eliot accepts the truth of this statement: "For the Christian there is no choice. Education is from top to bottom religious, or it is not education." [35] In a review in *The Criterion,* he states that "true" education should, among other ends, "develop a wise and large capacity for orthodoxy, to preserve the individual from the solely centrifugal impulse of heresy." [36] Furthermore, education should be controlled by priests: "I mean that the hierarchy of education should be a religious hierarchy. The universities are too far gone in secularization." [37]

As for equality of educational opportunity and the "democratisation of education," we have this passage from the highly praised *Notes towards the Definition of Culture*:

It is right that the exceptional individual should have the opportunity to elevate himself in the social scale and attain a position in which he can exercise his talents to the greatest benefit of himself and of society. But the ideal of an educational system which would automatically sort out everyone according to his native capacities is unattainable in practice; and if we made it our chief aim, would disorganise society, by substituting for classes, élites of brains, or perhaps only of sharp wits. Any educational system aiming at a complete adjustment between education and society will tend both to restrict education to what will lead to success in the world, and to restrict success in the world to those persons who have been good pupils of the system. The prospect of a society ruled and directed only by those who have passed certain examinations or satisfied tests devised by psychologists is not reassuring: while it might give scope to talents hitherto obscured, it would probably obscure others, and reduce to impotence some who should have rendered high service. Furthermore, the ideal of a uniform system such that no one capable of receiving higher education could fail to get it, leads imperceptibly to the education of too many people, and consequently to the lowering of standards to whatever this swollen number of candidates is able to reach.[38]

Eliot's program, whatever we may think of its inhumanity, might have applied to a nineteenth-century world where the son of a coal miner becomes himself a coal miner, where the daughter of a mill hand's wife herself goes to the mill, and where only the sons of Cambridge and Oxford men are themselves so educated. But that world was dying even in the nineteenth century, and after 1918 was dead. The strict class society, based on birth and wealth, which Eliot enjoys so much in Dr. Joad's description of life at Balliol College (quoted in the *Notes*), is becoming in England a thing of the past. It is almost pathetic that in 1949 Eliot should be deploring a situation in England that had passed from the stage of a project to limited operation. The famous public school of Harrow now receives secondary school boys from thirteen to eighteen. Eliot was horrified by the proposal "that the public schools should be taken over by the State and used as boarding schools to accommodate for two or three years the intellectually abler secondary school boys from the ages of sixteen to eighteen." [39]

This statement from the *Notes* can be amplified by his lengthy comments in a Church of England weekly, *The Guardian,* in 1950, where he discusses Clause No. 27 of the Lambeth Report on Education: "The Conference holds that the Church should press for the best educational opportunity everywhere for all, without racial distinction and without privilege for wealth."

Without presuming to interpret what the bishops were thinking when they wrote this clause, but taking into account the accepted use of the terms among educators in England, I think "without privilege for wealth" describes the now current practices in England for admission to the academic high schools and universities: that if a school or college can admit, say, 200 students, the admission will be decided in the first place on the basis of competence to profit by the proposed education. After this initial selection, the problem of paying for that education will be considered. "Without privilege for wealth" simply means that a student, unable to obtain admission in the regular way, will not be jumped over abler applicants because his father has the money to pay for his education. So much should be obvious.

Eliot, however, takes it as discrimination against those parents who wish to further their children's education and are able to pay for it. He says nothing about the children's ability for further education (for wealth's main privilege comes in advanced schooling). "The good education, in the usual sense, is very largely provided by parents who have saved especially for this purpose, or restricted their expenditure in other ways, in order to do the best they can for their children." [40]

To confuse the issue still more, Eliot throws in the false lead of pocket money: "I do not see how we can limit the term here to gross excess of wealth, since, even were persons in this position more numerous, there is a point beyond which money will not buy a 'better education'; it will only provide irrelevant trimmings; and excessive spending power in the hands of a schoolboy or undergraduate might even be an obstacle to his getting a good education." [41]

Let us now look at Eliot's ideas on marriage. In 1917, when he was twenty-nine, *"Lune de Miel"* ("Honeymoon") appeared. The revolting images conjured up in this piece suggest the pornographic titterings of an adolescent over risqué intimacies. A similar salacity characterizes *"Dans le Restaurant,"* in which an old waiter recounts his first sexual experiences as a child of seven. The honeymoon couple find themselves in a miserable flea-ridden hotel, and

Ils restent sur le dos écartant les genoux
De quatre jambes molles tout gonflées de morsures.
On relève le drap pour mieux égratigner.

(They lie on their backs, knees wide apart—
Four flabby legs all swollen with bites;
They lift up the sheet, the better to scratch.)

Here, then, in the early poems, Eliot's feeling for the relationship between men and women is offensively negative. It is expressed in that reverse face of adolescent romanticism, adolescent pornography.

Has this negative attitude changed over the years? In form yes, in essence no, to judge from the latest evidence in his play *The Cocktail Party*. The rejection of wholesome family relationships is now expressed in cynical terms. And the expression is given not to a stupid or comic character but to the chief character of the play, Dr. Harcourt-Reilly, who represents, if not the Voice of God, at least the mature voice of Eliot. The following views are therefore intended to be taken seriously and with respect by the audience.[42]

In marriage, says Eliot-Reilly, all that a couple can hope for is to be contented that they are

Two people who know they do not understand
each other,
Breeding children whom they do not understand
And who will never understand them.

Nor is this an isolated example. In his philosophical *Idea of a Christian Society* (1939), Eliot gives some advice to the ordinary man and woman trying to raise a small family with two or three children, and suggests what he considers desirable alternatives. We can almost hear the tone of Reilly (Eliot's literary alter ego), interpreter of the Will of God, saying, "It would perhaps be more natural, as well as in better conformity with the Will of God, if there were more celibates and if those who were married had larger families." [43]

In no play, poem, or prose work, does Eliot show that he has any concept of fulfilled love between a man and woman. The warm human relationships possible in life are all overlooked; life is seen as a boring routine of "birth, copulation, and death." What is for the majority of people the most ennobling experience in life, the glory and dignity of married love, is never mentioned. We might be tempted to ask why and perhaps to feel sorry for one who betrays such loneliness and frustration.

Still more disquieting is Eliot's lack of sympathy with minority groups. Often in the midst of obscure or difficult passages, there are (as with Ezra Pound) expressions which savor strongly of anti-Semitism. So we find in the early poems (1920) caricatures of Jews:

> Rachel née Rabinovitch
> Tears at the grapes with murderous paws

and in "Burbank with a Baedeker: Bleistein with a Cigar," Bleistein has

> A saggy bending at the knees
> And elbows, with the palms turned out,
> Chicago Semite Viennese.

And here the hostility becomes fascistic: in Venice

> The rats are underneath the piles.
> The jew is underneath the lot.
> Money in furs. . . .

And there is what can only be taken as a gratuitous slur on Jews in a reference to Karl Marx. Eliot's epithet "Jewish" does not identify Marx as an economist, as would such expressions as "classically trained" or even "bookish." "I wish that I had taken Hegel more seriously in my youth, but like many people I was caught napping; I never expected that Hegel, having been inverted by a Jewish economist for his own purposes, should come back again into favour." [44]

About the same time, in the year that Hitler came to power and started to "remedy" what Eliot considered undesirable, he was stating in his own person on the public lecture platform the inflammatory proposition that "reasons of race and religion combine to make any large number of free-thinking Jews undesirable. . . . And a spirit of excessive tolerance is to be deprecated." [45]

These quotations and the charges of anti-Semitism have rarely been discussed. Some pundits have brushed them aside as youthful indiscretions, although Eliot was forty-four when he made the last comment. Since then, Eliot has taken care to avoid any such direct expression of his feelings. In 1939 he was advocating the "quota" system in education: "The personnel will inevitably be mixed . . . The mixture will include persons of exceptional ability who may be indifferent or disbelieving; there will be room for a proportion of other persons professing other faiths than Christianity." [46]

This is a very frank statement in support of the notorious *numerus clausus* system by which only a percentage of Jews is admitted to some universities and which in some institutions governs the appointment of teachers. It is, of course, the current and only partly concealed form of anti-Semitism. Negroes[47] and Italians receive occasional digs from Eliot, though sometimes softened with patronizing adjectives, as in the following: "Civilization might just disappear everywhere: though we hope that Italians will go on singing their operas superbly and providing excellent cream-ices." [48]

In 1949 Eliot takes his stand against integration of cultures and against any expansion of minority groups—applicable, like the quota system, to others as well as Jews: "For it is an essential condition of the preservation of the quality of the culture of the minority, that it should continue to be a minority culture." [49] In the light of the previous quotations, this passage seems to indicate rather a concern for the preservation of the *majority* (Anglo-Saxon) culture uncontaminated by other influences. Such was surely the intent of the remark on the better chances for the re-establishment of "a native culture" in Virginia rather than in New England. For, said Eliot, in Virginia "You are farther away from New York; you have been less industrialised and less invaded by foreign races." [50]

These specific views on the world and the people in it, cannot be ignored or explained away; they are part of the whole literary personality. More serious still, however, is El-

iot's limited sympathy, amounting to a contempt for humanity. His anti-Semitism can then be seen as only the surface sore of a much deeper disease. How a man looks at any one group of people must be related to how he looks at all people in the world. The ugliness of Eliot's anti-Semitism is fully understood only when his antihumanism is recognized.

The Cocktail Party is full of examples of Eliot's antihumanism. For readers who have not seen the play a brief synopsis may be helpful. The chief characters include the Chamberlaynes, Edward, a presumably successful lawyer but inwardly disappointed man, and his nervously exhausted wife, who have come to the breaking point of their selfish, mutually eroding marriage; Celia Coplestone, a vivid, aspiring girl whose energies have thus far been wasted in a pointless courtship and a pointless affair with Edward; and Dr. Harcourt-Reilly who seems to figure as a spokesman for Eliot—and God—and whose role shifts between psychiatrist and that of home missionary to reconvert Christian heathen. Subsidiary characters include Celia's bore of a young man, Peter; Julia Shuttlethwaite, a garrulous, worldly, prying society woman; and a similarly worldly and repulsive British Foreign Office man named Alexander MacColgie Gibbs. The last two astound the attentive auditor after he becomes aware that they are presented not as Eliot's horrible examples of a decadent society but as examples of the souls salvaged by Reilly whose converts and secret aides they have become. The drama turns on Reilly's work as psychiatrist missionary in reconciling the Chamberlaynes to their hopeless inferiorities and to living with them and with themselves in dreary resignation; and in dispatching Celia, who has nobler stuff, into a convent and later on a mission where she will be privileged with the martyrdom of being eaten alive by ants while nailed to a crucifix.

This "martyrdom" is the outstanding example in the play of Eliot's callous disregard for people. The flippant way in which Celia's death is disclosed, first broached by the wise-cracks of Alex, the bright boy from the Foreign Office, about dining on monkeys; and the "almost inhuman levity" [51] of Reilly's description only makes "the horrible more horrible." Lavinia notices that Reilly's face "showed no surprise or horror At the way in which she died." She cannot comprehend that although Reilly knew about her, yet his "expression was one of . . . satisfaction!" Reilly's later explanation of his "satisfaction" is the most remarkable piece of mystic bunkum since Nostradamus:

> When I first met Miss Coplestone, in this room,
> I saw the image, standing behind her chair,
> Of a Celia Coplestone whose face showed the astonishment
> Of the first five minutes after a violent death.
> If this strains your credulity, Mrs. Chamberlayne,
> I ask you only to entertain the suggestion
> That a sudden intuition, in certain minds,
> May tend to express itself at once in a picture.
> That happens to me, sometimes. So it was obvious
> That here was a woman under sentence of death.
> That was her destiny. The only question
> Then was, what sort of death? *I* could not know;

> Because it was for her to choose the way of life
> To lead to death, and, without knowing the end
> Yet choose the form of death. We know the death
>   she chose.
> I did not know that she would die in this way,
> *She* did not know. So all that I could do
> Was to direct her in the way of preparation.
> That way, which she accepted, led to this death.
> And if that is not a happy death, what death is
>   happy?

The beliefs of a writer who is given such public acclaim are not a private problem, although even in the case of a private individual any man has the right to be shocked at perverse and retrogressive opinions. We weigh and consider the ideas or opinions of our friends and acquaintances and sit in judgment on their validity. Surely we must do the same with a writer. There is no such thing as poetic immunity.

Most readers who know perhaps only *Prufrock* or *The Waste Land* or "Tradition and the Individual Talent" (the best known of the essays) may be surprised and upset at this philosophy; yet it extends from the germ to the husk of Eliot's writings. Those who have read or witnessed *The Cocktail Party* may have seen beneath the conscious obfuscation which concealed the message of the play, and perhaps have felt that all was not well. The views on life we find in his poetry, with its restricted and limited imagery, in his drama, where all his characters are unloving and unlovable, and in his essays which are unashamedly reactionary, if not fasciscent, derive from an obvious hatred of people.

It should be more widely known that in these dithyrambs to Eliot we are asked to praise a writer who is avowedly antihuman.

In Eliot's writings we have an author who is without any faith in men. We have a mind that has substituted for a faith in man's powers the kind of religiosity which not only denies these powers but seeks to bind them, which not only wants to stop the clock of progress but to set it back. Eliot cannot or refuses to see dignity in man, and the wonderful possibilities which are man's. His persistent attacks on mechanization—senseless, illogical, like Mrs. Partington and her broom—try to hold back what can be a force for man's betterment. There is nothing of the recognition of the infinity of man's purpose in Eliot; no warmth, no kindness, no tenderness.

Eliot's attitude apparently rises from a despair with the world (reflected in *The Waste Land*), and a horrified retreat from the realities of life, too terrible, in this twentieth century, for a retiring spirit to bear. This withdrawal leads to a denial of objective reality, and an acceptance of some afterlife as the only reality. Life becomes the preparation for death. Everything that happens in our world is trivial and of no value, and man is very clearly marked with the burden of Adam. "I do not mean that our times are particularly corrupt: all times are corrupt." [52] Eliot has accepted as his own brand of orthodoxy the most narrow and rigid aspects of a Catholicism which rejoices in sacrifice and the death of the saints and ignores the positive *human* aspects of Christianity. Eliot's religion divides the world into sheep and goats, and colors all his thoughts and emotions with the

dread of Original Sin (the basis of whatever tragedy there is in *The Family Reunion* and *The Cocktail Party*). Thus in his "Second Thoughts about Humanism" (1929), Eliot upholds Hulme ("I agree with what Hulme says") : " 'what is important, is what nobody seems to realize—the dogmas like that of Original Sin, which are the closest expression of the categories of the religious attitude.' " [53]

In 1931 Eliot writes: "The real conflict is not between one set of moral prejudices and another, but between the theistic and atheistic faith; and it is all for the best that the division should be sharply drawn." [54] In *After Strange Gods,* in 1934, Eliot says: "I doubt whether what I am saying can convey very much to anyone for whom the doctrine of Original Sin is not a very real and tremendous thing." [55]

This emphasis ends with Eliot accepting a belief which very many Americans and British find incompatible with any God of love. Even strict theologians try to find exemptions from it, assigning a special corner of Purgatory to the little unfortunates. In his contribution to the anthology, *Revelation,* in 1937, Eliot wrote: "For instance, the doctrine of the damnation of unbaptized infants has been commonly rejected in recent times simply because it is repugnant. But the development of the state of mind to which this doctrine is repugnant must itself be examined before we can accept it with confidence; and the question of the repugnance of a doctrine is not the same as that of its truth." [56] Elsewhere in the same essay, Eliot writes: "The division between those who accept, and those who deny, Christian revelation, I take to be the most profound division between human beings. It does not merely go deeper than divisions by political faith, divisions of class or race; it is different in kind, and cannot be measured by the same scale." [57]

Eliot's verdict might well be extended to apply to his own writings (and the plays especially) after 1927. They cannot convey very much to anyone who does not accept his literal (rather than spiritual) interpretation of the Catholic Faith —Anglo-Catholic in England, elsewhere Roman Catholic.

In the following two chapters, I shall try to document exactly what Eliot's views are so that we shall understand the man whom so many accept as our great poet, critic, and dramatist. Further, I shall endeavor to show the effect of these views on Eliot's literary production, views which became established after Eliot became a naturalized subject of King—and Bishop. [58]

It is time for critics to re-evaluate the opinions and position of Eliot. It is time to ask, with the *Year's Work in English Studies*, "is not our generation tempted to take Eliot too seriously?" [59] It is time to ask whether his intransigeant religious and political opinions have not obtruded so much into his poetry, his drama, and his prose, that Eliot should perhaps no longer be considered a man of letters, but a propagandist.

THE
ELIOT
PHILOS-
OPHY

ELIOT'S PHILOSOPHY OF LIFE—WE MIGHT JUSTLY SAY PHILOSO-phy of death—pervades all his works but obtrudes more no-ticeably from about the end of the nineteen-twenties. Some-times it appears most clearly in his prose; at other times in the poetry or drama. Thus, as Miss Bradbook has pointed out:

> These earlier critical writings embody Mr. Eliot's own search as a poet for the material, no less than the prin-ciples, which would sustain him. His discovery of cer-tain poets is also a discovery of his own powers: the relation of the essays on 'Andrew Marvell' and 'The Metaphysical Poets' to *The Waste Land,* of that on 'Lancelot Andrewes' to *Song for Simeon* and *Journey of the Magi,* of that on *Dante* to *Ash Wednesday* are so direct that the criticism is often the best com-mentary on the poetry.[1]

The poetry conforms to Eliot's overall development. The earlier works are only occasionally overtly partisan. They do not present directly political or religious experiences, or even a tragic or serious view of life. The twelve poems in his first book, *Prufrock and other Observations* (1917), some of them supposedly written or drafted on his return to Harvard just before World War I,[2] are largely satirical, almost approaching *vers de société*. Here are found some of Eliot's best lines, barbed and amusing (if precious) observations. In *"The Boston Evening Transcript"*:

> The readers of the *Boston Evening Transcript*
> Sway in the wind like a field of ripe corn.

Or at the end of "Aunt Helen":

> The Dresden clock continued ticking on the mantel-piece,
> And the footman sat upon the dining-table
> Holding the second housemaid on his knees—
> Who had always been so careful while his mistress lived.

His little piece "Spleen" (Harvard, 1910)[3] gives a parallel to the later *Gerontion* or *Prufrock*:

> And Life, a little bald and gray,
> Languid, fastidious, and bland,
> Waits, hat and gloves in hand,
> Punctilious of tie and suit
> (Somewhat impatient of delay)
> On the doorstep of the Absolute.

In the "Five-finger Exercises" there is the amusing and revealing self-caricature:

> How unpleasant to meet Mr. Eliot!
> With his features of clerical cut,
> And his brow so grim
> And his mouth so prim
> And his conversation, so nicely
> Restricted to What Precisely
> And If and Perhaps and But . . .

That he could still write in this style as late as 1939 is seen
in the gay *Old Possum's Book of Practical Cats.* None of
this claims or is claimed to be great poetry. It is skillful and
clever minor verse recalling Chesterton or Dorothy Parker
or Lear or Austin Dobson.

The second early collection, *Poems* (1920), includes
"Gerontion", "Burbank with a Baedeker", "Sweeney among
the Nightingales", and nine other poems. Although later
in date than *Prufrock,* the attitude is one of adolescence
—delayed adolescence—in the choice of subject matter in
such poems as *"Lune de Miel"* and *"Dans le Restaurant."*

Then in 1922 comes *The Waste Land* which brought
Eliot into public notice and established his reputation. To
most younger readers of *The Waste Land* in the nineteen-
twenties and early thirties, the poem was a vivid and accurate representation of their barren world. It portrayed the
social disintegration and decay following the first War. Not
only are the upper classes morally bankrupt (Part II),
but the corruption has eaten into the middle classes
(Part III); the lower classes, too, have become impregnated

with a sense of futility (Part II). London—and not only its Bridge—was falling down. Louis MacNeice has described the impact of this poem in his account of "Eliot and the Adolescent":

> *The Waste Land*, needless to say, was the poem in this book which most altered our conception of poetry and, I think one can add, of life. . . . It is possible that at the age of eighteen we knew, however unconsciously, more about waste lands than most earlier generations did—or than any adolescent ought to know. Possible . . . but what is certain is this: to have painted the Waste Land so precisely, that those who had never to their conscious knowledge been there could so fully recognize it at first sight and at every subsequent meeting could find it still as real or more so, was the feat of a great poet.[4]

This subjective picture of the postwar world of the twenties was not at the time taken as preaching any message. Indeed, in reading *The Waste Land,* we should never know *why* it is a waste land or what precisely we should do to restore it to fertility. Even the ritual symbol of fertility has been excised. *The Waste Land* became a symbol of decadence in a period of crisis, "a kind of doldrums," [5] in which, he had said elsewhere, "we have no settled and satisfactory arrangement of society." [6]

It was not until seventeen years after its first appearance that Cleanth Brooks, in his *Modern Poetry and the Tradition,* came forward with an entirely new interpretation of *The Waste Land,* generally accepted since as "the most thorough exegesis." [7] He proposed that *The Waste Land* was not a poem of disillusion, a signature tune of the lost generation, but a poem of affirmation in the Christian religion. He may have got the germ for this idea from a hint in Eliot's *Thoughts after Lambeth,* (1931): "When I wrote a poem called *The Waste Land* some of the more approving critics said that I had expressed the 'disillusionment of a generation,' which is nonsense. I may have expressed for them their own illusion of being disillusioned, but that did not form part of my intention." [8]

For seventeen years, then, with all the attention that had been directed on the poem, the critics had failed to comprehend it; and Brooks dismissed them thus: "Though much has been written on *The Waste Land,* it will not be difficult to show that most of its critics misconceive entirely the theme and the structure of the poem." [9] Yet Brooks' interpretation and Eliot's own statement seem rather to be hindsight to justify the theological position Eliot had arrived at by 1931.

From about 1925, religion begins to dominate the poetry. Apart from *The Hollow Men* (1925), five "Ariel" poems (1927, two in 1928, 1930, 1931) a few minor poems (largely from *The Criterion*), the main work of 1925 to 1935 is *Ash Wednesday* (1930). "Burnt Norton" (the first of *Four Quartets*) appeared in the 1935 *Collected Poems,* along with the choruses from *The Rock* (1934), an ecclesiastical pageant. But between 1935 and 1950, of poems (as distinguished from poetic drama), Eliot has written only the three quartets (1940, 1941, 1942). These last poems are deeply religious, and not only express Eliot's personal search for belief, but set out the formal doctrines of the Church.

A fact which is often disregarded is that Eliot has written comparatively little poetry and that his production is sporadic. There is, indeed, apart from the *Four Quartets,* very little poetry after 1930, when Eliot's reputation had become established. His chief collections of poetry are these:

Prufrock and Other Observations (1917)	495 lines
Poems [including *Gerontion*] (1920)	415 lines
The Waste Land (1922)	433 lines
The Hollow Men (1925)	98 lines
Unfinished Poems [including *Sweeney Agonistes* (1926-7) 331 lines], *Minor Poems, Ariel Poems*	763 lines
Ash Wednesday (1930)	219 lines
Four Quartets (1943) [*Burnt Norton* 1934, *East Coker* 1941, *The Dry Salvages* 1941, *Little Gidding* 1942]	876 lines

Also in verse are the choruses in *The Rock* (1934), and the three poetic dramas.

It would appear that as Eliot's interest in formal religion increases, and as he finds himself more and more impelled to present his theological views on the state of the world, his productivity—and, some would argue, his ability—as a poet declines. Eliot, incidentally, was content in 1927 to call himself "a minor poet," [10] but by 1943 he admits he is a "good" poet.[11] The increasing interest in theology after about 1930 is reflected in the increasing number of polemical and sociological essays.

It is significant that those essays which deal for the most part with literary criticism were collected in 1932 as *Selected Essays,* subtitled *1917-1932,*[12] and that they have frequently been reissued without change (the latest edition is 1949). In all the following fifteen years (1932-1947) his literary essays were insufficient to form a parallel collection. Even in the *Selected Essays,* the religious-political trend is beginning to show itself; for example, in the essays "The Humanism of Irving Babbitt" (1926), "Second Thoughts about Humanism" (1929), and especially in the long essay, *Thoughts after Lambeth* (originally published as a separate book in 1931). Eliot also lets drop many gratuitous comments which clearly show his political leanings, such as, for example, his evaluation of Thomas Hobbes, a seventeenth century forerunner of modern thought, in the essay on "John Bramhall": "Thomas Hobbes was one of those extraordinary little upstarts whom the chaotic motions of the Renaissance tossed into an eminence which they hardly deserved and have never lost." [13]

For the most part, then, after 1930, philosophical and religious essays predominate. There are a few shorter works —*The Use of Poetry* (1933), *The Music of Poetry* (1942), *What Is a Classic* (1945)—which are not so directly theological. But the major works are exclusively concerned with religion and its place in the modern world—*After Strange Gods* (1934), *The Idea of a Christian Society* (1939), *Notes towards the Definition of Culture* (1949).

In *After Strange Gods* (first presented as a series of lectures) Eliot says, "I am uncertain of my ability to criticise my contemporaries as artist, I ascended the platform of these lectures only in the role of moralist." [14] *The Idea of a Christian Society* is offered as "a slight outline of what I conceive to be essential features of this society," [15] the Christian Society, that is, which Eliot would like to see throughout the world. In the *Notes,* Eliot, denying for the record that his purpose is, "as might appear from a casual inspection of the table of contents, to outline a social or religious philosophy," claims only "to help define a word, the word *culture*." [16]

Here Eliot notes how he has used his prestige as poet to obtain an audience for his religio-political views. If, he says, we all had more time and opportunity for the "exchange of ideas and information with men of distinction in other walks of life," there would be fewer books, "and we should not find the tendency—of which this essay provides one example—for those who have acquired some reputation, to write books outside the subject on which they have made that reputation." [17] This statement is, in fact, a repetition of the admission made in the early *The Idea of a Christian Society:* "The subject . . . is urgent because it is fundamental; and its urgency is the reason for a person like myself attempting to address, on a subject beyond his usual scope, that public which is likely to read what he writes on other subjects." [18] Writing for *The New English Weekly,* Eliot expressed the same position in somewhat more open language, when he was deriding H. G. Wells:[19] "When one had got sufficiently established, then one might be free, either to devote oneself to a work of literary art, or to preach openly to a public which is docile and respectful to success." [19] Surely, this is a valid description of Eliot's own work for these past twenty years.

These three books each show an increasingly conformable trend away from his position of the twenties, when Eliot was a literary rather than a political force. Then, Eliot called attention to the corruption of modern society; now he is silent. In *The Idea of a Christian Society,* for example, even as late as 1939, he made the pertinent observation: "We are being made aware that the organisation of society on the principle of private profit, as well as public destruction, is leading both to the deformation of humanity by unregulated industrialism, and to the exhaustion of natural resources, and that a good deal of our material progress is a progress for which succeeding generations may have to pay dearly." [20]

Yet by 1949, discussing imperial expansion, a development usually linked to the "principle of private profit," Eliot found whatever wrong in it due to "religious failure." Of imperialism itself, he writes: "To point to the damage that has been done to native cultures in the process of imperial expansion is by no means an indictment of empire itself, as the advocates of imperial dissolution are only too apt to infer." [21]

With similar convenient blindness, Eliot misinterpreted fascism as it appeared in Germany and Italy merely as a form of extreme nationalism:

> In Italy and in Germany, we have seen that a unity with politico-economic aims, imposed too violently and too rapidly, had unfortunate effects upon both na-

tions. Their cultures had developed in the course of a history of extreme, and extremely sub-divided regionalism: the attempt to teach Germans to think of themselves as Germans first, and the attempt to teach Italians to think of themselves as Italians first, rather than as natives of a particular small principality or city, was to disturb the traditional culture from which alone any future culture could grow.[22]

In the same book, Eliot refers to "fascist doctrine," as merely asserting "the absolute authority of the state"—a definition which would fit every known society, except that dreamed of by anarchists, and which holds true for America as well as socialized England. "The economic organization of totalitarian states," he calmly declares, "is not in question." [23]

At one time, Eliot's ideal society seemed to depend on a *via negativa* or religious withdrawal. This is apparently the setting of *Ash Wednesday* with its emphasis (especially in Part III) on purgation, detachment, and illumination. At the end of *Thoughts after Lambeth* (1931), deploring the contemporary corruption of society, he writes: "The World is trying the experiment of attempting to form a civilized but non-Christian mentality. The experiment will fail; but we must be very patient in awaiting its collapse; meanwhile redeeming the time: so that the Faith may be preserved alive through the dark ages before us; to renew and rebuild civilization, and save the World from suicide." [24]

His latest position, however, seems to depart from quietism and comes closer to an active clerico-fascism, based on a strict class society, dominated by his church, with very limited movement between classes. He postulates government by those "whose responsibility was inherited with their affluence and position." Admission into this Platonic utopia, although technically open to "rising individuals of exceptional talents" not born into it, would be in fact carefully regulated by denying to the rest that education which might possibly evoke the "exceptional talents":

> On the other hand, to be educated above the level of those whose social habits and tastes one has inherited, may cause a division within a man which interferes with happiness; even though, when the individual is of superior intellect, it may bring him a fuller and more useful life. And to be trained, taught or instructed above the level of one's abilities and strength may be disastrous; for education is a strain, and can impose greater burdens upon the mind than that mind can bear. Too much education, like too little education, can produce unhappiness.[25]

Even religion, which in *Thoughts after Lambeth* was to revitalize society, has now become a tool for politicians: "Any religion, while it lasts, and on its own level, gives an apparent meaning to life, provides the framework for a culture, and protects the mass of humanity from boredom and despair." [26]

Eliot's concern with religion and politics, which led him from poetry to prose, also led from poetry, which in modern times has always had a limited audience, to drama, and latterly to film. Here, bidding for more public attention, he used his position as the poet of *The Waste Land* to obtain a hearing in the theatre for his political views. With the exception of the "Sweeney" fragments (whose two basic themes are taken up in *The Family Reunion* and *The Cocktail Party*), Eliot's career in drama began only a number of years after his conversion from Unitarianism to Anglicanism. This switch, with its potentially wider (but still limited) audience, had long been contemplated by Eliot. In 1928 he was already searching for "a new form of verse which shall be as satisfactory a vehicle for us as blank verse was for the Elizabethans." [27]

In his presidential address to the Poets' Theatre Guild in 1949, Eliot, whose earlier *Murder in the Cathedral* had taken its subject from the past, describes his efforts to reach a modern audience. To this end he discarded the chorus and adopted plays of contemporary life, dealing with "men and women we know, in the usual clothes that they wear today, in the same perplexities, conflicts and misunderstandings that our acquaintances get involved in." [28] But while the setting changed to contemporary cocktail society, the subject matter has not changed. The propaganda of Thomas' sermon in *Murder in the Cathedral* is not unlike that of the later plays.

In the two modern plays, *The Family Reunion* and *The Cocktail Party,* the teaching is formulated, not for prospective saints, who are therefore to be reverenced, but for ordinary men. The sole progress shown is an ability to coat the pill of dogma of an archbishop's sermon with the flavors of fashionable sophistication. The propaganda technique is somewhat more subtle, and the message, as applied to daily life, more corrupting. Now it calls on people to make the best of an evil situation instead of trying to remedy the evils. For Eliot, apparently there is no decency in the living man; that must wait until he has become a martyr.

The Cocktail Party presents people who see the world going to pieces, want to avoid worrying about it, and find relief from the worries they cannot evade in a vague mysticism. The surface theme in general is popular and safe: sex and religion—a spicy situation of who is sleeping with whom, and who gets bored first, and the consolation that there is organized religion to fall back on. Three quarters of the play is drawing-room farce; the remaining quarter (which contains the moral) depends on the acceptance of the doctrine of Original Sin and of Grace and Atonement.

Celia, the girl whom Harcourt-Reilly dispatched to her martyrdom, introduces these technical terms, "sin," and "atonement," for no apparent reason, since she was brought up in upper-middle-class paganism. We might well ask, Why does she need a psychiatrist? After the break-up of her affair with Edward, she reflects on the "treasure" she had hoped to find in it. When that falls far short of her expectations—when she finds nothing, in fact—she says, "Why do I feel guilty at not having found it?" If Celia had said "frustrated," it would have been more in keeping with the way people's minds work and with her situation. Does Eliot mean that everyone who is frustrated in love must consult a psychiatrist—or a priest? What happens is that the psychiatrist-priest convinces Celia she is guilty (of something or other) and, by so persuading her of guilt, is more readily able to send her away to work for the Church.

The mystical conjurations of *The Cocktail Party* echo *The Family Reunion*—"scolding hills," "valley of derision," "the labyrinth," "the quicksand," "the circular desert," "stone passages," "smoky wilderness"—and culminate in the fantastic runes mumbled by characters one is supposed to admire for their spiritual insight. In *The Family Reunion* the spectacle of two university-trained women incanting "the pilgrimage of expiation" round a small portable table with a birthday cake with lighted candles ("At each revolution they blow out a few candles, so that their last words are spoken in the dark") is matched in sheer nonsense only by the spectacle in *The Cocktail Party,* which is totally unprepared for, of a London medical specialist, an interfering old socialite, and the young man from the Foreign Office offering this "libation":

> May the holy ones watch over the roof,
> May the Moon herself influence the bed.

Eliot's unquestioning acceptance of authority and obedience in religion and (by reflection) in political affairs consistently developed from his diagnosis of twentieth-century society. Contemporary society is suffering from "moral laziness and evasion" (1933),[29] from ennui, boredom, or spiritual sloth; it is a society "worm-eaten with Liberalism" (1934).[30] "The great majority of people are neither one thing nor the other, but are living in a no man's land" (1939).[31] (A no man's land once described as a waste land?)

What is going to happen? There are three possibilities for our civilization, says Eliot:

My thesis has been, simply, that a liberalised or negative condition of society must either proceed into a
gradual decline of which we can see no end, or
(whether as a result of a catastrophe or not) reform
itself into a positive shape which is likely to be effectively secular. . . . But unless we are content with the
prospect of one or the other of these issues, the only
possibility left is that of a positive Christian society.[32]

In 1922, Eliot, though a return to religion is hinted at in
The Waste Land, was primarily concerned, as I have noted
(p. 24), with portraying the state of society, a society where
the standards of art and culture were being insidiously de-
pressed by "the steady influence which operates silently in
any mass society organised for profit,"[33] and in which
"much in our system is not only iniquitous, but in the long
run unworkable and conducive to disaster."[34] After the appearance of *Poems 1909-1925,* he ceased to be interested in
depicting the modern dilemmas of the middle and upper
classes, and became very positively identified with the third
possibility he envisaged in the passage quoted above. "You
must be either a naturalist or a supernaturalist."[35] Elsewhere, Eliot contrasts the two ways, characterizing follow-
ers of naturalism as exponents of "secularism," who are
"simply unaware of, simply cannot understand the meaning of, the primacy of the supernatural over the natural
life."[36] Eliot expands on the meaning of materialism, naturalism, or secularism. It is "an exaggerated faith in human reason";[37] it is "the belief in human perfectibility";[38]
it is the aim which seeks "prosperity in this world for the
individual or the group."[39]

Throughout his writings one finds this contempt for life in this world. In *Murder in the Cathedral,* for example, the contempt goes beyond the ascetic's renunciation of those ephemeral pleasures held up by the First Tempter:

> Fluting in the meadows, viols in the hall,
> Laughter and apple-blossom floating on the water,
> Singing at nightfall, whispering in chambers. . . .

Looking back over his previous life, Thomas finds only hollowness in his activities, such as

> Delight in sense, in learning and in thought,
> Music and philosophy, curiosity.

The Four Tempters, anticipating the "bitter tastelessness of shadow fruit" of *Little Gidding,* turn on Thomas and tell him the truth about himself:

> Man's life is a cheat and a disappointment;
> All things are unreal,
> Unreal or disappointing:
> The Catherine wheel, the pantomime cat,
> The prizes given at the children's party,
> The prize awarded for the English Essay,
> The scholar's degree, the statesman's decoration.
> All things become less real, man passes
> From unreality to unreality.

This rejection of reality is reiterated in Eliot's last plays, perhaps because he thinks that in the theatre his audience will accord that "willing suspension of disbelief" and, for a couple of hours, accept his theology. In *The Cocktail Party* there are hazy discussions of reality. Peter, for example, asks,

"What is the reality of experience between two unreal people?"

But what does "unreal" mean? In what sense are the people "unreal"? Not existing on earth but in someone's imagination (in which case they must have had an existence some time to be re-created in someone's mind)? Existing only as "ghosts" (and what does it mean if his audience does not believe in ghosts)? Unreal like Baudelaire's unreal city? Phony in the colloquial sense, having no personality, or too artificial in thoughts and manners? Or unreal in the Aristotelian sense?

But so long as the injunction to accept the unhappiness of the world we live in is put across, the logical use of language is not important: "the world I live in seems all a delusion," cries Celia. Talking to her lover Edward after the debacle, and seeing him in a new light as an apron-tied, tired, middle-aged man, she tries to place her unhappiness against the larger significance of "reality":

> That is not what you are. It is only what was left
> Of what I had thought you were. I see another
>   person,
> I see you as a person whom I never saw before.
> The man I saw before, he was only a projection—
> I see that now—of something that I wanted—
> No, not *wanted*—something I aspired to—
> Something that I desperately wanted to exist.
> It must happen somewhere—but what, and where
>   is it?

Earlier, Celia describes her infatuation for Edward—"a private world of *ours*"—which crashed, as

> A dream. I was happy in it till today. . . .
> Perhaps the dream was better. It seemed the real
>   reality,
> And if this is reality, it is very like a dream.

In the earlier *The Family Reunion,* the principal figure, Harry, also cannot live at peace with the world around him because the world's reality is unbearable:

> You have gone through life in sleep,
> Never woken to the nightmare, I tell you, life
>   would be unendurable
> If you were wide awake.

And the world—

> The things I thought were real are shadows, and
>   the real
> Are what I thought were private shadows.

Harry has come to see that "What you call the normal Is merely the unreal and the unimportant."

The message of the plays, especially *The Family Reunion,* is exactly the same as that of the polemical prose: the world we live in is not reality. Nor is this approach surprising from one who has rejected *in toto* any rational or humanist explanations of existence, having chosen the alternative in what he has described as "two and only two tenable hypotheses about life: the Catholic and the materialistic." [40]

When Eliot speaks of Catholicism, he speaks as a member of the Church of England, which he thinks (and probably most Anglicans agree) is the Catholic Church in England. For in England "the main cultural tradition has for several centuries been Anglican," so that, as far as England is concerned, Roman Catholics, who are "in a more central European tradition than are Anglicans," [41] are actually outside the English cultural tradition.

But Eliot's interpretation of the theological position of the Church of England is by no means that held by a majority of her clergy and certainly not by a majority of the laity. Eliot can hold religious and political beliefs which for most Anglicans are more Roman than Catholic, and remain a member of that communion, because, as he himself observed, "the Church of England itself has comprehended wider variations of belief and cult than a foreign observer would believe it possible for one institution to contain without bursting." [42]

Had Eliot remained in America, he might by now be a Roman Catholic. Some of his views, especially the more recent, have an identity with Roman Catholicism, as John Chapman in the New York *Daily News* pointed out: "I suppose that *The Cocktail Party* is basically Roman Catholic." [43] His acceptance of certain dogmas and practices, his interpretation of history, and, most especially, his advocacy of political activity by the hierarchy show a decidedly ultramontane orientation. In 1934 he thanked a prominent Jesuit for criticism of his book; [44] in 1935 he admitted, "With Mr. [G. K.] Chesterton [the Roman Catholic writer] I naturally have sympathies which I did not have twenty-five years ago." [45] This trend had been obvious to a few critics for some time, and in 1933, John Strachey, the present British Minister of War, was asking: "Why cannot he be, at any rate, a real Catholic? Becoming an Anglo-Catholic must surely be a sad business—rather like becoming an amateur conjurer." [46]

Having thrown in his lot with a rigid "Catholicism" (Eliot, as an Anglican, is no doubt considered schismatic, perhaps heretic, by Roman Catholic standards), Eliot makes no secret of his desire to see a world controlled by his Church: "By 'the Church's message to the World' you might think that what was meant was only the business of the Church to go on talking. I should like to make it more urgent by expanding the title to 'the Church's business to interfere with the World.'"[47] He includes, in his *The Idea of a Christian Society,* an Appendix dealing with this design: "Now, *how* is the Church to interfere in the World?" [48]

In the first place, the state should recognize, and be guided by, only one religion, Catholicism. "The national faith must have an official recognition by the State, as well as an accepted status in the community." [49] In another essay, forgetting his Manichean statement that both the Catholic and the materialistic hypotheses are tenable, he describes himself as committed to the belief that "the Christian world order is ultimately the only one which, from any point of view, will work." [50] He adds that his system "shall recognize the place of ecclesiastical authority." [51] Eliot has elsewhere explained that "if the idea of a Christian society can be grasped and accepted, then it can only be realised, in England, through the Church of England." [52] Eliot does not say what would be the organization to receive "official recognition by the State" in countries other than England, but, from his theological position, we can legitimately assume the Roman and Orthodox Catholic Churches would be the only bodies to fulfill his doctrinal requirements.

Eliot rejects the willingness to accept different views—the principle on which American and British democracy rests. How can the following quotation be reconciled with the form of government we profess to honor: "I think that the virtue of tolerance is greatly overestimated, and I have no objection to being called a bigot myself." [53] To avert any suspicion in the reader's mind that this quotation is wrenched from its context, I offer this longer quotation from *The Idea of a Christian Society*; the sting of this extract is in the tail:

> What is often assumed, and it is a principle that I wish to oppose, is the principle of live-and-let-live. It is assumed that if the State leaves the Church alone, and to some extent protects it from molestation, then the Church has no right to interfere with the organisation of society, or with the conduct of those who deny its beliefs. It is assumed that any such interference would be the oppression of the majority by a minority. Christians must take a very different view of their duty.[54]

Not only should the State recognize one religion—which in turn would recognize the State and guide it—but, following the pattern of such clerico-fascist states as Spain, only one religion is to be tolerated. If, says Eliot, you want a Christian Society (as he does), you cannot allow "congeries of private and independent sects." [55] "Any programme that a Catholic can envisage must aim at the conversion of the whole world. The only positive unification of the world, we believe, is religious unification. . . ." [56] As a loyal Anglican, Eliot continues this last sentence, "by which we do not mean simply universal submission to one world-wide ecclesiastical hierarchy, but cultural unity in religion—which is not the same thing as cultural uniformity."

Sometimes there seem to be doubts whether men and women should be made to fit the system or vice versa. At one point in *The Idea of a Christian Society,* Eliot seems to be advocating a hypocritical conformity on his inhabitants of the Christian Society: "The rulers, I have said, will, *qua* rulers, accept Christianity not simply as their own faith to guide their actions, but as the system under which they are to govern. The people will accept it as a matter of behaviour and habit." [57] Such dualism is hard to accept from a genuinely religious person. How Eliot would have attacked such sentiments in the mouths of rationalists like Polybius, Lucretius, Montesquieu, or Voltaire, who actually held that religion was something to be enforced by the rulers but believed only by the people they ruled!

On the other hand, Eliot does not clearly indicate whether conformity to his religion would be enforced or not on the inhabitants of his future society. At one time, he seems to envisage a small minority of tolerated non-conformists—"there will be room for a proportion of other persons professing other faiths than Christianity." [58] At another time, he seems to favor pogroms, considering—"any large number of free-thinking Jews undesirable. . . . And a spirit of excessive tolerance . . . to be deprecated." [59]

Yet all, conforming or not, will accept the control, down to the minutest detail of their personal, everyday lives, which the omnipotence and omnipresence of the state religion would ensure. "Our religion imposes our ethics, our judgement and criticism of ourselves, and our behaviour toward our fellow men." [60] All questions of morality will be decided by the Church. "Morality rests upon religious sanction; and . . . the social organization of the world rests upon moral sanction." [61] Where medical or religious views might conflict, as, for example, on birth control, "Spiritual guidance should be imperative; and it should be clearly placed above medical advice." [62] If there is ever to be a censorship, "it ought to be at Lambeth Palace," [63] the residence of the Bishop of London. Or again: "In matters of dogma, matters of faith and morals, it [the Church] will speak as the final authority within the nation." [64] Foreign affairs will be taken over by Catholics: "I believe also that Catholics should, in any question of foreign relations, be able to feel a sympathy with foreign points of view which is much better worth having and more effective than diffuse goodwill." [65]

This view is expanded in Eliot's editorial in *The New English Weekly,* which gives fulsome praise to the official archdiocesan publication, *The Tablet*: "nowhere else in the weekly press do we see world affairs discussed with so much penetration." [66]

Eliot, too, places an unusually high value on practices which, while not condemned in the Church of England, are more characteristic of the Church of Rome. In *The Idea of a Christian Society,* for example, he writes, "I cannot conceive a Christian society without religious orders, even purely contemplative orders, even enclosed orders;" [67] adds a sneer at Coleridge, who "quite failed to recognise the enormous value which monastic orders can and should have in the community;" [68] and, continuing his praise of monasticism, gives an unconscious description of what he may have hoped *The Cocktail Party* would achieve. Speaking of the general acceptance of Christianity in his ideal society, where men and women, however, would be "not individually better than they are now," he says: "But their holding the Christian faith would give them something else which they lack: a *respect* for the religious life, for the life of prayer and contemplation, and for those who attempt to practise it." [69]

Eliot's penchant toward Rome comes out in his interpretation of history, an example of which I have already given (pp. 9-14). The quotation that "the western tradition has been Latin, and Latin means Rome" is pedantically amplified:

> There are countless testimonies of art and thought and manners; and among these we must include the work of all men born and educated in a Catholic society, whatever their individual beliefs. From this point of view, the separation of Northern Europe, and of England in particular, from communion with Rome represents a diversion from the main stream of culture. To pronounce, upon this separation, any judgment of value, to assume that it was a good or a bad thing, is what in this investigation we must try to avoid; for that would be to pass from the sociological to the theological point of view.[70]

Here, for all his scientific talk, Eliot is actually making a value judgment, and one based on mere quantity. By stressing the volume, "the countless testimonies," of art produced

in the Roman Catholic tradition, Eliot is implying a lesser quantity (or quality) produced in other, Protestant, traditions; and to follow this view would mean that Northern Europe suffered culturally from its separation from Rome.

Yet we know that in England the flowering of culture (with the possible exception of architecture) did not take place until after 1550. Eliot consequently seeks to avoid this comparison (which would question his whole theory of a Roman tradition) by disclaiming any need for judgment. Nevertheless, he later reaches the conclusion that a decline of Roman Catholic traditions would mean a decline in English culture: "just as the culture of Protestant dissent would perish of inanition without the persistence of Anglican culture, so the maintenance of English culture is contingent upon the health of the culture of Latin Europe, and upon continuing to draw sustenance from that Latin culture." [71] He offers no evidence for this theory; it seems far different from a theory of continental "influences" and ignores the considerable reciprocating influences of English on continental culture.

In like fashion, Eliot tries to show that national cultures flourish better if there is a force making for "uniformity of belief and practice." The only organized force answering that description is the Roman Catholic Church. Eliot concludes, "And without a common faith, all efforts towards drawing nations closer together in a culture can produce only an illusion of unity." [72]

Such opinions as the foregoing may clearly be stamped clerical. How far the majority of practicing Catholics and Christians would be prepared to accept them as being wholly representative of Catholicism and Christianity is another matter. If they are admitted as typical, then the survival and influence of the Christian religion cannot be explained by rational means. The truth is that Eliot has neglected the humanitarian and human aspects of Christianity, which from the first made it a living force. Christianity could not have gone far if it had offered nothing beside "mortification and sacrifice."

Eliot has given his Christianity a very marked political twist. To the rulers, Christianity is merely "the system under which they are to govern"; for those governed, Christianity is "a matter of behaviour and habit." One is tempted to wonder whether or not Eliot's incomplete presentation of Catholicism is more political than religious. In fact, of one of Eliot's interpretations of his religion, *The Idea of a Christian Society,* one reviewer, Father Maurice B. Reckitt, said: "This represents no true idea of a Christian society." [73]

Reading his *Notes towards the Definition of Culture,* one is forced to conclude that Eliot has little faith in Christianity. He ascribes many wonderful achievements to it in the past, but is vague about its present and future values. "The culture of Europe has deteriorated visibly within the memory of many," he tells us, and he can see "no reason why the decay of culture should not proceed much further." [74] And even active Christians, he notes elsewhere, "can have very little hope of contributing to any immediate social change." [75] With his loss of genuine faith in the value of Christianity goes a concomitant loss of hope and charity:

> I said to my soul be still, and wait without hope
> For hope would be hope for the wrong thing: wait
>   without love
> For love would be love of the wrong thing.

The great religious authors in England are great because they possess this trio of faith, hope, and charity. They have never been inhuman; they have always filled their writings with human aspirations, human experience, human imagery, and have fought for people's betterment here on earth. Milton, perhaps the greatest English religious poet, always opposed the clericality so dear to Eliot. His oration on receiving his degree at Cambridge is a magnificent early specimen of confident faith in the new man:

> So at length, gentlemen, when universal learning has once completed its cycle, the spirit of man, no longer confined within this dark prison-house, will reach out far and wide, till it fills the whole world and the space far beyond with the expansion of its divine greatness. Then at last most of the chances and changes of the world will be so quickly perceived that to him who holds this stronghold of wisdom hardly anything can happen in his life which is unforeseen or fortuitous. He will indeed seem to be one whose rule and dominion the stars obey, to whose command earth and sea hearken, and whom winds and tempests serve; to whom, lastly, Mother Nature herself has surrendered, as if indeed some god had abdicated the throne of the world and entrusted its rights, laws, and administration to him as governor.[76]

In another great and devoutly religious poet, Langland, we find similar strength. It is the same with Bunyan. There is an awareness of wonder, a realization that man's present knowledge is infinitesimal in comparison to the knowledge yet to be learned.

Fascist-tending opinions reveal themselves quite as clearly. With his predilection for the reactionary, it is perhaps surprising that Eliot never went beyond his preference for "royalism" in politics to an open advocacy of fascism, as did his friend Pound. Eliot's comments were never direct. In 1925, he wrote a short "Dialogue," where one character (apparently presented with respect) says, "The best we can hope for, the only thing that can save us, is a dictator." [77] This piece appeared just before the British General Election. In 1928 Eliot did comment on *The British Lion,* the organ of the British Fascists: "The aims set forth in the statement of policy are wholly admirable." [78] He commented favorably on Nazism as late as October, 1939: "But totalitarianism can retain the terms 'freedom' and 'democracy' and give them its own meaning: and its right to them is not so easily disproved as minds inflamed by passion suppose." [79] Expanding this statement in a footnote, Eliot said of a certain General J. F. C. Fuller, who called himself a "British fascist": "From my point of view, General Fuller has as good a title to call himself a 'believer in democracy' as anyone else." [80] Black-shirted fascism was never fashionable in England, although there was sympathy for fascist ideology, made concrete by the Anglo-German Fellowship, which, as late as 1938, included among its members some sixty Conservative Members of Parliament and Peers of the House of Lords.[81]

Some of Eliot's other pronouncements in favor of fascist ideas must have seemed shocking to many Englishmen. Perhaps no outcry was raised because at the time so few people knew about them. The circulation of his magazine, *The Criterion,* was under a thousand when he wrote in March, 1937, "But Mr. Day Lewis suffers from the weaknesses of most Englishmen of his belief. There is nothing, for these people, to be said for fascism." [82]

By 1937, more and more British were becoming critical of Hitlerism, and opposition in the university circles was growing with the knowledge that scholars were being exiled and imprisoned and that the once proud German academic journals had grossly deteriorated. Consequently, there was general academic support for the lead taken by Oxford in refusing to send delegates to the Bicentenary celebrations of the University of Göttingen. Here is Eliot's shocked and pseudo-naive reaction, tucked away in the pages of *The Criterion* (July, 1937): "It seems hardly credible, at the moment of writing, that the motive of the authorities of Oxford University in deciding not to send representatives to that celebration could have been to express disapproval of the German Government. But it is to be feared that their action may be so interpreted in Germany, and (pending an explanation) may be so interpreted here too." [83]

In *The Idea of a Christian Society,* published just after the outbreak of the war with Germany, there are at least half a dozen passages, which if they do not actually condone fascist ideology, at least—under the pretext of fairmindedness —present it in a favorable light. This reasonable statement, for example, would have some appeal to most readers:

> We are in danger of finding ourselves with nothing to stand for except a *dislike* of everything maintained by Germany and/or Russia: a dislike which, being a compost of newspaper sensations and prejudice, can have two results, at the same time, which appear at first incompatible. It may lead us to reject possible improvements, because we should owe them to the example of one or both of these countries; and it may equally well lead us to be mere imitators *à rebours,* in making us adopt uncritically almost any attitude which a foreign nation rejects.[84]

The note he appends, however, reveals how this disarming thesis should be interpreted—namely, a disposition, if not prejudice, toward fascism: "one of the main tenets of the Nazi creed" is acceptable. Eliot refers us to a report made by Miss Bower of the Ministry of Transport at a conference of the (British) Civil Service Clerical Association. Miss Bower who "moved that the association should take steps to obtain the removal of the ban (i.e. against married women Civil Servants) said it was wise to abolish an institution which embodied one of the main tenets of the Nazi creed— the relegation of women to the sphere of the kitchen, the children and the church." [85]

On this Eliot comments as follows with an at first hesitantly apologetic air, as if striving to be "fair."

[1] The report, by its abbreviation, may do less than justice to Miss Bower, but I do not think that I am unfair to the report, in finding the implication that what is Nazi is wrong, and need not be discussed on its own merits.
[2] Incidentally, the term 'relegation of women' prejudices the issue.
[3a] Might one suggest that the kitchen, the children and the church could be considered to have a claim upon the attention of married women?
[3b] or that no normal married woman would prefer to be a wage-earner if she could help it?
[4] What is miserable is a system that makes the dual wage necessary.[86]

Observe how, in his opening sentence, Eliot appeals to the semantic concept of the *word* as not denoting the *thing*. By this plea he sets aside all the connotations of the word Nazi which happen to be inconvenient to a propagandist of re-action and which are by no means as irrelevant here as Eliot would make it appear. The second sentence again cries "label." Few sociologists except those already committed to a contrary view by the requirements of their creed would justify a ban on married women working. Sentence three with its scholarly "Might one suggest," is another evasion. It sets up a straw man, for Miss Bower does not say what Eliot imputes to her, that kitchen, children, and church have no claim on married women. Moreover, judging by the characters in his poems and plays, and by his published opinions on marriage, I wonder if Eliot has the remotest idea of what a "normal married woman" does prefer. The last sentence quickly tries to gain general support by an unarguable comment on the inadequacy of men's wages, but in fact it reinforces his over-all position against married women working.

Here are some further quotations from *The Idea of a Christian Society* offered only with this query: How dangerous would the Nazis have considered any well-known "democratic" writer who agreed that fascism was efficient; that it revived a "way of life" for the Germans; and that the main objection to it was not the "oppression and violence and cruelty" but its "paganism"?

> We conceal from ourselves, moreover, the similarity of our society to those which we execrate: for we should have to admit, if we recognised the similarity, that the foreigners do better. I suspect that in our loathing of totalitarianism, there is infused a good deal of admiration for its efficiency.[87]

> What we are seeking is not a programme for a party, but a way of life for a people: it is this which totalitarianism has sought partly to revive, and partly to impose by force upon its peoples.[88]

> The fundamental objection to fascist doctrine, the one which we conceal from ourselves because it might condemn ourselves as well, is that it is pagan. There are other objections too, in the political and economic sphere, but they are not objections that we can make with dignity until we set our own affairs in order. There are still other objections, to oppression and violence and cruelty, but however strongly we feel, these are objections to means and not to ends.[89]

Still more interesting, I think, are those opinions less recognizable as clerical or fascist in tendency, but nevertheless strongly reactionary. These unlabelled views crop up in prose and drama, and are generally concealed by a veneer of man-of-the-world polish, so that their insidiousness has already gone to work before their political partisanship is realized.

Several instances occur in *The Cocktail Party* (1950). This "bitter pill," as the *Manchester Guardian*[90] termed its political message, is, of course, coated so that it will not immediately offend. Under the brittle Noel Coward icing is the long advocated program, propounded more fully and openly (without the obfuscation of visions and crucifixions) in the *Notes towards the Definition of Culture,* published only one year before the play was produced. In both the play and the *Notes* one finds many applications of Eliot's clerico-fascism to the problems of everyday life. Two in particular may be noted.

One of Eliot's favorite theses is an echo of what Burke and all historians of the organic school were saying a hundred or a hundred and fifty years ago—Modern society is corrupt, but don't try to change it. Ever since *The Waste Land* described the feelings of despair of the lost generation, Eliot has been critical of Western civilization. As late as 1939 he was saying, "And it does not require a Christian attitude to perceive that the modern system of society has a great deal in it that is inherently bad." [91] Even then, Eliot was suggesting the need of changes in society to remove what was "inherently bad." Eliot, speaking as his particular brand of Christian, naturally wanted a society to conform with his interpretation of the faith, but he was prepared to accept change and a new order of society:

> My primary interest is a change in our social attitude, such a change only as could bring about anything worthy to be called a Christian Society. That such a change would compel changes in our organisation of industry and commerce and financial credit, that it would facilitate, where i[t] now impedes, the life of devotion for those who are capable of it, I feel certain.[92]

In 1950, Eliot is still cynically critical. What have people to live for, he asks in the play. "What have they to go back to?"

> To the stale food mouldering in the larder,
> The stale thoughts mouldering in their minds.
> Each unable to disguise his own meanness
> From himself, because it is known to the other.

Ours is a world "of lunacy, violence, stupidity, greed." But now, although his views of Western society remain unfavorable, he shies away from the idea of reform or change, advocated eleven years earlier. His prescription in 1950 is, for the average run-of-the-mill man and woman (not the elect suitable for martyrdom), acceptance of this *status quo* of violence and greed. Edward, interpreting Counselor Reilly's advice to Lavinia, says:

> Lavinia, we must make the best of a bad job.
> That is what he means.

Is this acceptance the best way out? Not necessarily, but "It is a good life." Reilly underlines this view: "The best of

a bad job is all any of us make of it." In the *Notes towards
the Definition of Culture,* Eliot likewise affirms his cynicism
toward contemporary cultural "retrogression":

> We can assert with some confidence that our own pe-
> riod is one of decline; that the standards of culture are
> lower than they were fifty years ago; and that the evi-
> dences of this decline are visible in every department
> of human activity. I see no reason why the decay of
> culture should not proceed much further, and why we
> may not even anticipate a period, of some duration, of
> which it is possible to say that it will have *no* cul-
> ture.[93]

Yet what does Eliot suggest we do about it? Here, as in
the play, he expresses no hope that any considerable change
can be effected. Just let things be, he says:

> For the rest, we should look for the improvement of
> society, as we seek our own general individual im-
> provement, in relatively minute particulars. We cannot
> say: 'I shall make myself into a different person'; we
> can only say: 'I will give up this bad habit, and en-
> deavour to contract this good one.' So of society we can
> only say: 'We shall try to improve it in this respect or
> the other, where excess or defect is evident; we must
> try at the same time to embrace so much in our view,
> that we may avoid, in putting one thing right, putting
> something else wrong.' Even this is to express an aspi-
> ration greater than we can achieve; for it is as much or
> more, because of what we do piecemeal without un-
> derstanding or foreseeing the consequences, that the
> culture of one age differs from that of its prede-
> cessor.[94]

Another belief of Eliot's that philosophically bolsters the forces of reaction is: Man should not trouble himself about the evils of the world. This moral is both implicit and explicit in *The Cocktail Party,* particularly in the account of Edward and Lavinia Chamberlayne's reception of the news of Celia's crucifixion. Since he rejected her, Edward feels he is in some way responsible for her decision to enter a religious order which led to her death. He is not fully convinced by Reilly of the paradox that this death was the way of life for Celia—it would be interesting to know just who is convinced that Celia's death was a triumph. Edward complains, "It's the waste that I resent." Later, Reilly answers him:

> As for Miss Coplestone, because you think her
>   death was waste
> You blame yourselves, and because you blame
>   yourselves
> You think her life was wasted. It was triumphant.
> But I am no more responsible for the triumph—
> And just as responsible for her death as you are.

He reiterates:

> Let me free your mind from one impediment:
> You must try to detach yourself from what you still
>   feel
> As your responsibility.

A similar disregard for what happens to others appears earlier, before Celia has become a nun, and when Edward is still involved. He says to Reilly:

It's about the future of . . . the others.
I don't want to build on other people's ruins.

Reilly replies:

Your business is not to clear your conscience.
But to learn how to bear the burdens on your
conscience.
With the future of the others you are not concerned.

That the characters of the play are to be taken as symbols
for Everyman is a view strengthened by the *Notes*. "With
the future of the others you are not concerned" here takes
the form: Public affairs are not the concern of everybody:

We may assume, I think, that in a society so articulated
the practice of politics and an active interest in public
affairs would not be the business of everybody, or of
everybody to the same degree; and that not everybody
should concern himself, except at moments of crisis,
with the conduct of the nation as a whole. In a healthily *regional* society, public affairs would be the business
of everybody, or of the great majority, only within
very small social units; and would be the business of a
progressively smaller number of men in the larger
units within which the smaller were comprehended.
In a healthily *stratified* society, public affairs would be
a responsibility not equally borne: a greater responsibility would be inherited by those who inherited special advantages, and in whom self-interest, and interest
for the sake of their families ('a stake in the country')
should cohere with public spirit.[95]

What Eliot calls regionalism another might call parochialism—the confining of interest to the immediate surroundings and problems. But this limitation is not to apply to the wealthy, who have "a stake in the country." As usual, it is baldly assumed, as during the English Revolution of 1642 and the American Constitutional Convention of 1787, that the interests of propertied people are the interests of the country. The events of those times showed at least the possibility that the interests of the country run counter to the interests of an entrenched aristocracy.

Eliot will not admit even that representation by suffrage is an axiom inherent in democratic thinking. Discussing "Universal Suffrage" in *The Criterion,* he states with customary disregard of documentation what is otherwise an assumption: "It is a commonplace that the increase of the electorate, in Britain, is the destruction of Democracy; that with every vote added, the value of every vote diminishes." [96]

One of the major aims of the *Notes* is to reaffirm the need for a class society, where class is determined by money and birth. The rule of landed hereditary classes only emphasizes the difficulty of change: "The governing élite, of the nation as a whole, would consist of those whose responsibility was inherited with their affluence and position, and whose forces were constantly increased, and often led, by rising individuals of exceptional talents." [97] The belief is repeatedly spelled out: "A real democracy is always a restricted democracy, and can only flourish with some limitation by hereditary rights and responsibilities." [98]

Eliot not only approves a type of social structure now obsolete, but resists any attempt to educate men and women so that they would be better informed about public affairs. In discussing a *Report of the Consultative Committee on Secondary Education,* he takes issue with the statement (made in 1939 before the outbreak of war): "Democracy is now challenged, and the duty of citizenship in a democracy renders it essential that all should be taught to understand and to think to the best of their ability." With this aim it is difficult to quarrel. Eliot gives his conception of the way most readers would interpret the sentence: "But to most readers, I fancy, the sentence I have just quoted would immediately suggest understanding, and thinking about politics and economics." So far so good. Eliot, however, continues: "But these are matters which few can understand, and fewer still can do anything about: the great majority of people should be taught to understand what they can understand, and to think about those things to which their thinking can make some difference." [99]

This opinion had been given in almost identical words nearly ten years earlier in an editorial in *The Criterion*: "And in a democracy, it is essential that people should understand the matters upon which they are exhorted to make decisions, and that they should not be called upon to decide upon matters which they do not understand." [100]

In the essays the implications of these themes are clear enough, although they may not hit a theater audience immediately. The effect of the play, however, comes to the same thing. It advocates a program of clerical-inspired reaction just as much as do the more outspoken praises of a hierarchical state from any hack politician. Man is isolated—

> We must also remember
> That at every meeting we are meeting a stranger.

If man is isolated, he therefore cannot hope to work in a group with other men for the realization of his aims, and consequently can accomplish very little. Tied in with this belief is that of man's predestination (a favorite with Eliot). Such a theory enfeebles any urge for change. Edward expresses this spirit of the tired acceptance of inevitable evil:

> I see that my life was determined long ago
> And that the struggle to escape from it
> Is only a make-believe, a pretence
> That what is, is not, or could be changed.

How comforting is such a philosophy to vested interests in an age of decay.

The *Notes* also provide examples of hidden propaganda on other topics. Eliot has expressed reactionary views on education over a long period of time, from his "Modern Education and the Classics" in 1933 and his "Education in a Christian Society," a supplement to the *Christian News Letter* (1940), and in editorials in the same weekly (1942), to the early essays in the *New English Weekly,* rearranged to form a chapter contributed to the anthology *Prospect for Christendom* (1945), and again arranged to form Chapter I of the *Notes towards the Definition of Culture* (1949).

Eliot wrote very freely for the *Christian News Letter,* for whose small and discreet circle of readers no disguise was needed:

> I cannot help suspecting, however, that it is possible
> that education, in the meaning of the word which it

has in contemporary society, is over-valued—by being contrasted simply with the *absence of itself,* and not with anything positive. With this thought in mind, I think that the claims of 'equalisation of opportunity' and the 'democratisation of education' ought to be scrutinised very carefully. I trust no one will suppose me to be a defender of a social order and an educational system based upon income—the best thing to be said for which is that it manages to keep up some *pretence* of being based upon breeding. . . . But for the great majority, 'opportunity' may be no more than opportunity to aim to excel (or at least keep their end up) at whatever the people with whom they associate think admirable. I am not the enemy of opportunity, I only say that in providing opportunity you are assuming a very grave responsibility.

Equalisation of opportunity, then, and democratisation of education, are in danger of becoming uncritical dogmas. They can come to imply, as an ultimate, a complete mobility of society—and of an atomised society. I mean by this that many of those who hold those two principles may be unconsciously carrying them over from nineteenth-century liberalism—and in so far as they spring from liberalism they may end in totalitarianism. It is to think of the individual in isolation, apart from family and from local milieux, as having certain intellectual and sensitive capacities to be nurtured and developed to their full extent; and of a system of education as a vast calculating machine which would automatically sort out each generation afresh according to a culture-index of each child. The result might be to produce a race of spiritual nomads.[101]

Significant in the first paragraph is Eliot's acceptance, in spite of carefully worded denials and restrictions, of "breeding" as a criterion, when he knew perfectly well that in the nineteenth century (and earlier) breeding was for all practical purposes limited to those with money. The 1945 essay, "Cultural Forces in the Human Order," formed the first chapter of the later *Notes*,[102] where Eliot is still upholding those earlier views on the desirability of limited education.

To clinch his points, Eliot wishes to "make sure that no one received *too much* education, limiting the number treated to 'higher education' to a third (let us say) of those receiving that treatment today." [103] Eliot is here referring to education in England in 1933, when the number of students at all British universities combined was only about fifty thousand out of a population of fifty million. Eliot's prescription applied in America in 1951 would limit the number of students, graduates and undergraduates, to fifty thousand in our 150 million!

And this reactionary nonsense is being praised in a country that prides itself on the educational opportunities it affords! It is possible that the influence of Eliot as a man of letters may persuade those people in American university circles in a position to determine the direction of education to accept and to put into practice his views. This is why Eliot's overblown reputation is a matter of concern as much for the man who has never read a word by him as for the scholar. For both, if the adulation of Eliot in the United States persists, are likely to find their lives subjected to some degree to the ideas of this self-named "bigot." [104]

A typical example of the way in which Eliot's ideas are picked up (consciously or unconsciously) is the speech of William J. Wallin, former Chancellor of the New York State Board of Regents, on March 28, 1949, at a dinner given for General Dwight D. Eisenhower, before 365 Columbia graduates. Mr. Wallin made four main points. I give pertinent extracts from his speech,[105] and the parallel references from Eliot.

1. THE STATE SHOULD NOT PROVIDE HIGHER EDUCATION FOR ALL THOSE WHO DESIRE IT.

W. J. Wallin:

In the field of higher education there is a widespread belief and tenet that government has a duty to guarantee and provide everyone who desires it an opportunity for higher education, even in the professions.[106]

T. S. Eliot:

So long as we consider 'education' as a good in itself of which everyone has a right to the utmost, without any ideal of the good life for society or for the individual, we shall move from one uneasy compromise to another.[107]

2. INCREASED EDUCATION WILL LEAD TO LOWERING EDUCATIONAL STANDARDS.

W. J. Wallin:

There is the danger, already measurably apparent, that with the large numbers to be educated the quality of the education afforded will be greatly diluted.

T. S. Eliot:

Furthermore, the ideal of a uniform system such that no one capable of receiving a higher education could fail to get it, leads imperceptibly to the education of too many people, and consequently to the lowering of standards to whatever this swollen number of candidates is able to reach.[108]

3. FEDERAL OR STATE AID DESTROYS EDUCATIONAL FREEDOM.

W. J. Wallin:

The danger to tax-supported institutions, and even to tax-aided institutions, that the policies, politics and ideology, perhaps the control of a strong-willed executive or a politically minded legislature, will be imposed upon them and their real freedom destroyed.

T. S. Eliot:

There is also the danger that education — which indeed comes under the influence of politics—will take upon itself the reformation and direction of culture, instead of keeping to its place as one of the activities through which a culture realises itself.[109]

4. TOO MUCH EDUCATION LEADS TO UNHAPPINESS AND FRUSTRATION.

W. J. Wallin:

We are likely to educate, particularly in the post-graduate area, many more men and women than can earn a living in the field in which they have chosen to be educated, and too often anywhere else, and we shall find that, embittered with their frustration. . . .

T. S. Eliot:

On the other hand, to be educated above the level of those whose social habits and tastes one has inherited, may cause a division within a man which interferes with happiness. . . . And to be trained, taught or instructed above the level of one's abilities and strength may be disastrous.[110]

Going a step further than Mr. Eliot, Mr. Wallin let a cat out of the bag. His last sentence continued thus: "embittered with their frustration, these surplus graduates will turn upon society and the Government, more effective and better armed in their destructive wrath by the education we have given them." This is the real reason for the attack on increased educational opportunities. With education, people will no longer be content with poor standards of living but will demand a better way of life. If the society in which they were educated cannot meet their needs, then they may even seek to change it. Eliot does not explain what he means by "disastrous," but he says everything which leads to Mr. Wallin's conclusions; for Eliot knows that an uneducated nation, or a nation of men educated only for the jobs to which their social station has fitted them, is the more likely to accept the control by an elite governing class and entertain no thoughts of replacing it. In the society conceived by Mr. Wallin, there is no prospect of jobs for these educated young men and women; his world has no use for their talents.

A religion or philosophy limiting the very education which, says Eliot, can give a "fuller and more useful life" to every individual, is obviously not a means to this fuller life but a substitute. In his writings Eliot seems to have been unable to find such a life in this world and, in consequence, he hates the world. Rejecting and rejected by this natural world which is our reality—psychologists tell us the two go together—he passes to a belief in a supernatural world. This is not an isolated phenomenon among certain types of intellectuals. Eliot has very accurately portrayed the feeling, when he ascribes it to Baudelaire: "He rejects always the purely natural and the purely human; in other words, he is neither 'naturalist' nor 'humanist'. Either because he cannot adjust himself to the actual world he has to reject it in favour of Heaven and Hell, or because he has the perception of Heaven and Hell he rejects the present world: both ways of putting it are tenable." [111]

One does not have to subscribe to the tenability of the second suggestion to agree that this passage is a good account of Eliot's own development: "he cannot adjust himself to the actual world." He is constantly stressing the vanity of the world and opposing to it as the only true "reality" some supernatural state. All mystics, if they meditate long enough on the things they want, come to believe the imaginings of their own hearts to be "true."

Eliot makes no secret of his opinions, but it is a valid question to ask him and those who, without too much reflection, may accept his beliefs: "In what country of the world, at the present time, are these theories put into practice?" There is one obvious answer: Franco's Spain. If Eliot and his admirers want to live under clerical fascism, there is little comment to be made.

Eliot has the right, of course, to hold these views. But a critic has the corresponding right to draw attention to these beliefs which mirror the man. It is important to call them to the attention even of those who consider that in a poet craft considerations come first. It is an axiom of literary criticism that as a man is, so are his writings. Eliot himself at one time agreed with this view, when in his essay "Religion and Literature" he wrote:

And if we, as readers, keep our religious and moral convictions in one compartment, and take our reading merely for entertainment, or on a higher plane, for aesthetic pleasure, I would point out that the author, whatever his conscious intentions in writing, in practice recognizes no such distinctions. The author of a work of imagination is trying to affect us wholly, as human beings, whether he knows it or not; and we are affected by it, as human beings, whether we intend to be or not.[112]

If Eliot kept his convictions to himself, and did not publish them in his writings, then this monograph need not have been written. However, when any writer uses his writing to promote a society where only his interpretation of utopia will be allowed, then the critic has a duty to expose the propaganda in the writing and, if he thinks fit, to oppose it.

Over all Eliot's writings hovers his contempt for human beings—because, as we know them, they are part of the physical world. Man, to Eliot, is a sorry thing. "The majority of mankind is lazy-minded, incurious, absorbed in vanities, and tepid in emotion, and is therefore incapable of either much doubt or much faith." [113] His contempt comes out in crotchety comments upon their lack of education or lack of perspicacity—"readers—most of them quite uneducated";[114] "the public is not very well qualified for discriminating between nostrums";[115] at the moments when the public's interest is aroused, "the public is never well enough informed to have the right to an opinion";[116] "the more serious authors have a limited, and even provincial audience, and the more popular write for an illiterate and uncritical mob." [117] Eliot's religion or philosophy limits the education of the people and then complains that the people are uneducated. It is all part of a facile contempt for people—both those for whom he writes his poems and plays, and those about whom he writes.

It is not that Eliot's people are inherently contemptible; they become contemptible under Eliot's treatment—sneering at their failings and ignoring their strengths. It matters not whether one is a London typist on a holiday on the river and another Queen Elizabeth drifting in state down the Thames: each is of an earth that is dirty, sterile, mean. Where is the character we can respect in *The Family Reunion* or in *The Cocktail Party*? Celia possibly—but we cannot admire her gullible submission to Reilly.

The people of Eliot's early poems are equally obnoxious: there is hardly one (Pippit perhaps excepted) whom a healthy-minded person would choose as his friend. There is only negative sensibility—not disillusion but revulsion; not the love of truth but the gloating in untruth. There is no recognition of beauty but an absorption in dirt and filth. Eliot is so fearful of the generative process that he can see only ugliness in sex. In *"Lune de Miel,"* which I have previously mentioned, there is no response to the decent joy and freshness of young married love; all that the disgusted Eliot can see are sweaty legs covered with flea-bites. There is the other tid-bit of *"Dans le Restaurant."* Eliot, with his superior irony, exhorts us to remember "the Platonic hint that nothing in this world is wholly serious—that 'nothing' including of course the prolongation of one's own existence in the world." [118]

It is all very well to rationalize this fondness for the repellent as "a negative pursuit of beauty," and for Eliot to claim the example of Dante as justification. Much of his subject matter and imagery remains revolting to those who hope for a world free from the landmarks of Eliot's country:[119] the one-night cheap hotels, decayed houses, bats with baby faces, drying combinations, female smells in shuttered rooms, the drooling of an old man's mouth, protozoic slime, rancid butter, frittered lives, squalid deaths. And yet Eliot talks glibly about one poem being "more memorable" than a second—Why? Because "there is greater beauty in the subject matter." [120]

Nor is it any mitigation to say that his characters are as they are because the poem or play demanded them. It is the author who decides the plot and draws the characters. And I believe Eliot is fully cognizant of what he is writing. Long ago, he said: "The fiction that we read affects our behaviour towards our fellow men, affects our patterns of ourselves. When we read of human beings behaving in certain ways, with the approval of the author, who gives his benediction to this behaviour by his attitude toward the result of the behaviour arranged by himself, we can be influenced towards behaving in the same way." [121]

How rat-ridden is Eliot's world is forcibly recalled by using Matthew Arnold's old touchstone—a few lines of great poetry, such as Hamlet's lines on the boundless potentialities of man:

What is a man,
If his chief good and market of his time
Be but to sleep and feed? a beast, no more.
Sure, he that made us with such large discourse,
Looking before and after, gave us not
That capability and god-like reason
To rust in us unused.

The philosophy of Eliot, as revealed by these quotations and illustrations from his work, can be summed up in one word: Anti-Humanism. It manifests itself in destructive hatred of the world and contempt for people. "In my end is my beginning" has adequately been spelled out by one commentator: "For just as man's purpose is set at his birth, so only at death does that purpose begin to be realized." [122] It is, after all, only natural that one who is an enemy of life should be concerned with death. He is a poet of death.

Eliot's philosophy is equally inimical to scientific methods and achievements—"But the circle of our understanding Is a very limited area"—and of all the processes of rational thought. Intuition and presentiment are held superior to ratiocination. Anti-humanism is the philosophy of one who, not able (for whatever reason) to face the realities of life or to accept the external objective world, counterfeits a world of his own, and tries to pass it off as the genuine thing. The kinds of beliefs which Eliot has propagated are in themselves sufficient to deny Eliot the place among first-rank authors which many critics have so hastily accorded him. No writer with such a limited range of sympathies can manifest that universal insight into and concern with all types of humanity which characterize the greatest.

A significant example of his aloofness and assumed superiority, both in regard to people and poetry, is Eliot's reply to the questionnaire sent to men of letters at the time of Franco's rebellion: "While I am naturally sympathetic [to the Spanish Loyalist government], I still feel convinced that it is best that at least a few men of letters should remain isolated and take no part in these collective matters" [123] —the expression of a personality which draws back from humanity, from the very material which, as a writer, he has to use in his creative works.

Eliot is not alone in this decadence. There are, in fact, other well-known authors who deny reality and try to stifle the natural desires of man to better his world. But the acclaim of greatness has not so readily been accorded to them —nor to contemporary British authors who have been more outspoken than Eliot in his "guarded affection for fascism," [124] such as Roy Campbell, Wyndham Lewis, or Evelyn Waugh. Yeats, with all his aberrations of cabalism, occultism, and spiritualism, was always warmly human, and in any case has never been granted recognition as more than a poet—an intellectual or moral leader—as has Eliot. Nor is the position of Ezra Pound as a poet, despite the continuing support of Eliot (who has written introductory prefaces for him), by any means assured.

No matter what motive leads them to their anti-human positions, genuine or false, such writers with their belittling of man are, in this century especially, all too easily used by the fascist-minded. It is in their service that today Eliot's writings exert an influence, perhaps because he half-disguises his views under a clerical cloak. In intellectual circles he has become the chief mouthpiece of reaction.

THE
ELIOT
WRITING

THE PROBLEM POSED BY THIS SUMMARY OF ELIOT'S PHILOSO-
phy—can we (in his own words) "judge and enjoy a man's
poetry while leaving wholly out of account all of the things
for which he cared deeply, and on behalf of which he
turned his poetry to account" [1]—was discussed at great
length in Eliot's series of lectures delivered at Harvard
(1932-1933), and published as *The Use of Poetry and the
Use of Criticism*. Here Eliot develops his statements on
the interrelation between ideas and literature, and in one
passage seeks to justify his "abhorrence" of certain poets
(like Milton or Shelley):

> When the doctrine, theory, belief, or 'view of life' pre-
> sented in a poem is one which the mind of the reader
> can accept as coherent, mature, and founded on the
> facts of experience, it interposes no obstacle to the

reader's enjoyment, whether it be one that he accept or deny, approve or deprecate. When it is one which the reader rejects as childish or feeble, it may, for a reader of well-developed mind, set up an almost complete check.[2]

Surely a writer who holds views such as those analyzed in the previous chapter, many of which must seem neither coherent nor mature, is risking that sympathy which he deems necessary from "as large and various a number of people as possible," [3] and is setting up checks for the enjoyment of his imaginative writings.

Eliot's writings approach stature only where they ignore or depart from his theological theories. This relation may be the reason why a large proportion of readers find more enjoyment in his earlier prose and in his early poems, where his irony and disillusion make no pretensions to being the greatest literature. Perhaps, when the man-scorning, life-hating prejudices in his work have been swept away and forgotten except as source material examples of intellectual perversity, *Old Possum's Book of Practical Cats* is the book that future generations will read and enjoy. Yet this is the one book the "experts" have ignored. It may be crammed with symbols, allusions, and quotations, but no critic has yet undertaken an exegesis. We are free to enjoy its subtlety of rhythms and sounds without referring to a footnote.[4] Eliot is best when his doctrine is least.

The corollary also holds true: Eliot's work is worst where there is most doctrine. His verse bogs down in quotations from the classics of mysticism, and in his own brand of catholicism. The drama is self-consciously obscurantist;

through his muddle of confused thought, he keeps pounding on the reader the theme of the insufficiency of man and the vanity of living. The characterization is two-dimensional, as in most of the medieval mystery and morality plays. Developments are not explained, and the situations are contrived to illustrate a thesis. In his prose, as elsewhere, there is contempt for communication; it is marked by obscurity, back-tracking, pontification, and downright deception.

In his later works, Eliot's religion or philosophy or politics (he makes no practical distinction among them) becomes more and more important. Such numerous direct and formal statements of a politico-religious point of view are unexpected in creative writing. The exact date at which Eliot became a preacher is difficult to determine. Indications are present in *The Waste Land* (poetry) in 1922. The sermonizing becomes overt in 1925 in *Ash Wednesday* (devotional verse). By 1931 it becomes blatant in *Thoughts after Lambeth* (prose). After about the middle of the twenties, Eliot gives his doctrines such rigid adherence that whatever he writes is forced to conform to the prescribed formula, whether or not it be suitable. Eliot has tried—to paraphrase one of his own well-known dicta—"to force, to dislocate if necessary," literature to fit his morality.

In his unswerving desire to have the Church "interfere" (pp. 48-49) with the world, he lets the Church interfere with his poetry, which is, after all, part of the world. His later verse particularly becomes so involved with specific dogmas that, while *understanding* is possible, appreciation is limited to those who share Eliot's tenets. It is curious that a writer, who sometimes admits communication as a goal of poetry, should restrict himself by the use of imagery and language so remote from most people living in this "neutral" society, who conform only "to the practices of Christianity on the occasions of birth, death, and the first venture into matrimony." [5] For Eliot does not refuse a large audience: "there is no doubt that a poet wishes to give pleasure, to entertain or divert people; and he should normally be glad to be able to feel that the entertainment or diversion is enjoyed by as large and various a number of people as possible." [6]

It must also occur to many people that Eliot's Christianity has little in common with the precepts of Christ; and that, for all its moral pretensions, the religion expressed in Eliot's works is always self-centered and negative. If the world be such a miserable place as he describes it, Eliot does little to make it any better. "The note of disdain and contempt for the masses," observes Harold Laski, "is omnipresent; and I call this a betrayal of culture, a form of intellectual treason, because it leaves those prisoners of the dark forces in society to whom it might have sought to communicate their way to emancipation." [7]

As poet, Eliot has kept paring his audience. From a coterie of knowledgeable aesthetes, he has whittled it down to an even smaller band of acolytes. *The Rock* in 1934 is an undisguised religious pageant, made to order, reminiscent of the occasional verse of Gower and Lydgate.

> What life have you if you have not life together?
> There is no life that is not in community,
> And no community not lived in praise of GOD.

> Even the anchorite who meditates alone,
> For whom the days and nights repeat the praise of
> GOD
> Prays for the Church, the Body of Christ incarnate.

Eliot has so filled most of his recent writing with dogma and doctrine; he has so increasingly employed specialized religious terminology, has so insisted on the cleavage between ritualistic Christians and the rest, that its essential appeal has become limited to ritualistic Catholics.

Ash Wednesday, the first of the religious poems (1925), presumes an audience thoroughly at home with ecclesiastical ritual. The central idea of the poem, the imagery and language, are permeated with Catholic beliefs. Eliot does not rely so much on the Anglican *Book of Common Prayer* for his imagery and diction, although there are some references to this source (e.g. "And let my cry come unto thee") as on private Latin prayers and the Roman Catholic liturgy. There are significant quotations from the *Ave Maria*, the *Salve Regina*, the Reproaches, the Canon of the Mass, the Sacrament of Penance, and the *Anima Christi*.

That this reliance on religious background was delimiting his potential public is generally allowed. It was admitted by such a staunch admirer of Eliot as Helen Gardner, who Babette Deutsch, in her review of Miss Gardner's book,[8] thought had weakened her case by "extravagant admiration" and assumption of Church of England dogmas as "the way, the truth, the life." Miss Gardner wrote:

> In *Ash Wednesday* Mr. Eliot, in Langland's fashion, employed phrases from the prayers and liturgies of

the Church. But it is doubtful whether these phrases fulfilled their proper function, except for a small minority of readers. I think they were felt as an irritant by the majority, to whom they brought no real associations of prayer and worship, but merely the suggestion of conventional religious phraseology.[9]

Miss Gardner adds a footnote to the passage, which, because it comes from a fellow Anglican, is all the more revealing for the later direction of Eliot's verse and for the difficulties it entails for a poetry reader outside the faith. Miss Gardner adds:

> The most remarkable demonstration I have had of this failure in communication in *Ash Wednesday* was at a tea-party, when a colleague said that the repetition at the close of Section III always suggested to him a drunk man coming home late at night and muttering to himself as he stumbled up the stairs. When someone present objected: 'But it is a phrase from the Canon of the Mass', he replied: 'How am I supposed to know that; it doesn't mean anything to me.' When someone else added: 'But surely you recognize it as coming from the New Testament?', he answered: 'Well, lots of phrases come out of the Bible ultimately.' Even for those who accept the Christian Faith, some of the phrases in *Ash Wednesday* have less than their full effect, for to feel their force one needs to be accustomed to use them in the same context as the poet. I have sometimes felt that only those presented on the occasion of their Confirmation with that popular manual of devotion, *St. Swithun's Prayer Book*, read *Ash Wed-*

nesday with a natural response to the poet's intention.[10]

So to appreciate *Ash Wednesday* one must have a manual of devotion (well thumbed) in one hand, and Eliot's text in the other. But Eliot knows well that most people, including churchgoing Christians, have a very slight acquaintance with Church literature. He complains that the most highly educated, whose professional need he thinks might suggest such acquaintance, know nothing. Commenting on the limitations of Professor Norman Foerster, Eliot wrote: "One can now be a distinguished professor, and a professional moralist to boot, without understanding the devotional sense of the word *vocation* or the theological sense of the virtue *humility*." [11] In the light of these comments, who, we might ask, can enjoy *Ash Wednesday?*

The same comment may be made on *Four Quartets,* but to a greater degree. The professedly religious terminology is almost as obvious as it is in *Ash Wednesday*, and a strictly Catholic creed is even more implicit in the poetry. "Burnt Norton" concludes with an appeal to St. John's Gospel and a reference to the Temptation in the Wilderness (which would probably be understood by all readers), and—what would not be immediately intelligible—a reference to St. John of the Cross (whom Eliot had quoted in the epigraph to *Sweeney Agonistes* in 1926: "Hence the soul cannot be possessed of the divine union until it has divested itself of the love of created beings"). St. John of the Cross is again drawn upon at the close of the third section. *East Coker* is an explanation of the Atonement and the Mystery of the Cross, along with the full Catholic doctrine of the Mass:

> The dripping blood our only drink,
> The bloody flesh our only food:
> In spite of which we like to think
> That we are sound, substantial flesh and blood—
> Again, in spite of that, we call this Friday good.

In *The Dry Salvages* there is the technical use of "Annunciation," and the Fourth Section (the lyric) is a Prayer to the Blessed Virgin Mary as Queen of Heaven:

> Repeat a prayer also on behalf of
> Women who have seen their sons or husbands
> Setting forth, and not returning:
> Figlia del tuo figlio,
> Queen of Heaven.

Mr. Eliot, as an Episcopalian, should know that what implies Mariology is, to members of his Church, at least irregular, if not heretical; and that many readers would be precluded, because of its dogma, from sympathetic consideration of this lyric (obviously intended seriously by the author, and not, as with a fifteenth-century poet, a verbal exercise where the author could substitute a very earthly mistress for the Queen of Heaven).

Of the "tremendous rhymed lyric of section four," Rajan believes that "People to whom it is not immediately impressive are unlikely to be convinced by a description of its subtleties." [12] In this way Rajan dismisses sincere students and lovers of poetry who are unable to have an immediate re-

sponse to this "religious phraseology." The delimited audience is stressed in the comments of another critic, who says
in all seriousness: "Finally, to understand *Four Quartets* we
need to live with them, and even to live by them." [13] Poetry
here, perhaps to Eliot's chagrin, has taken the place of religion.

Another defect in Eliot's poetry which can be attributed
to his religiosity is his imposed and second-hand perception.
He knows what he should believe according to his Catholicism, but finds it hard to vitalize that belief. Perhaps the
clearest illustration of this inability to convey his experience
occurs at the end of *The Waste Land* on pp. 135-139.
Eliot, through the eyes of Tiresias, has described his pilgrimage through the waste land, and comes to an affirmation of
his own ultimate salvation. If the experience has meant anything to him, Eliot should be able to find words of his own
to tell us about it—for that is the peculiar skill of a poet. Yet
at this significant moment, Eliot has to rely on the words of
others. In the same way, the experiences of others are drawn
upon throughout the *Four Quartets,* especially in *Little Gidding* with its key lines from Dame Juliana of Norwich's
Revelations and the anonymous *Cloud of Unknowing.* One
is reminded of a candidate for ordination who, having heard
of the necessity of receiving a "call", bones up on the auto-
biographies of evangelicals describing their "revelations" before he faces the Bishop's selection committee. The major
difference in Eliot's borrowings in the early and later poetry
is that in the latter his sources and analogues are from minor
writers and non-imaginative authors. Even as a literary
debtor he deteriorates.

It might further be remarked that in his poetry Eliot uses expressions from other poets to describe his spiritual life. In the plays the characters portrayed as undergoing spiritual crises evade the issue by asserting that their spiritual experiences cannot be expressed by words.

Eliot's first play, *Murder in the Cathedral* (1935), is based on the twelfth-century Archbishop of Canterbury, St. Thomas à Becket, who came in conflict with King Henry II in an attempt to resist what history has since judged to be progressive social changes. The play turns on the temptations of life and power and reason (as opposed to faith) which Becket might enjoy if he yielded. Becket withstands the tempters and subsequently meets martyrdom at the hands of knights who come to fulfil what they take to be the king's unspoken behest.

The play is free of the twentieth-century voodoo chants we are to find in *The Family Reunion* and *The Cocktail Party*. It removes the problem of salvation to the twelfth century and makes it concrete in an historical figure. But the major problem, the portrayal of a mystical change in a character, is not met. Thomas discusses a particular temptation with each of his four tempters and (like Harry in *The Family Reunion* that was to be Eliot's next play) becomes mysteriously clear in his own mind what course to adopt: "Now is my way clear, now is the meaning plain." But the audience is allowed no share in the revelation; it is kept as much in the dark as before; and Thomas's concluding speech does nothing to clarify the meaning.

In the second part of the play, Thomas says little and is slain by the king's knights almost at the opening of the act.

Eliot refers to the mystical conversion (so similar to Harry's in *The Family Reunion* and Celia's in *The Cocktail Party*) but what he means remains obscure:

> There is one moment,
> But know that another
> Shall pierce you with a sudden painful joy
> When the figure of God's purpose is made complete.

Even an audience of believers, watching a pageant in a cathedral, needs more enlightenment than this. All that Eliot tells us is that Thomas has some great secret:

> I have a tremour of bliss, a wink of heaven, a whisper
> And I would no longer be denied; all things
> Proceed to a joyful consummation.

What goes on in Thomas' mind, and what this secret is which gives him serenity to meet his death are not discussed. The sermon spoken in the course of the *play* gave Eliot another opportunity to explain what his acceptance as servant of God means. But the sermon, from the point of view of motivation, is useless. Its only dramatic function could be to reveal more of Thomas's thoughts and to make credible to a modern audience his acceptance of martyrdom. Presumably the idea of peace is Thomas's motivation, and this might explain his later action. But the sermon fails dramatically; what this Peace means is not explained. "But think for a while on the meaning of this word 'peace,'" says Thomas. ". . . Reflect now, how Our Lord Himself spoke of Peace."

He said to His disciples 'My peace I leave with you, my peace I give unto you.' Did He mean peace as we think of it: the kingdom of England at peace with its neighbours, the barons at peace with the King, the householder counting over his peaceful gains, the swept hearth, his best wine for a friend at the table, his wife singing to the children? These men His disciples knew no such things: they went forth to journey afar, to suffer by land and sea, to know torture, imprisonment, disappointment, to suffer death by martyrdom.[14]

To a modern theatre audience not necessarily predominantly Episcopalian and thus conditioned to these phrases, all that Thomas has said here is that this "Peace" does not mean freedom from war and freedom to pursue commerce without let. Thomas continues: "What then did He mean? If you ask that, remember then that He said also, 'Not as the world gives, give I unto you.' So then, He gave to His disciples peace, but not peace as the world gives." There is, however, no definition or explanation here of peace, and we may wonder, if Peace (with the capital) has nothing to do with peace (with the minuscule), why it is called peace at all. Structurally, the weakest part of this sermon (if we so take it in its literal sense) is that, not having clarified the conception but only given extracts from the Gospels, Eliot, after another page or so, assumes that he has done so, "Asking you . . . to remember what is that Peace which He brought." The women of Canterbury might well be disappointed in the inadequate help their Archbishop gave in what was to be his last sermon. There is much talk, but it gets nowhere. Certainly we of the twentieth century must feel cheated that so much time has been given to subjects which "the world cannot understand."

If, therefore, this "Interlude" has no dramatic function, why is it inserted? It seems that the play can best be considered as an ecclesiastical pageant, and that the sermon serves merely to give expression to tenets of the Christian Faith. Only a year before, in the prose *After Strange Gods* (1934), Eliot had been discussing the relation between tradition and orthodoxy, which he dramatized in the play. Here he demanded a resurgence of orthodox Catholic tradition as a solution to current problems:

> As we use the term *tradition* to include a good deal more than 'traditional religious beliefs', so I am here giving the term *orthodoxy* a similar inclusiveness; and though of course I believe that a right tradition for us must be also a Christian tradition, and that orthodoxy in general implies Christian orthodoxy, I do not propose to lead the present series of lectures to a theological conclusion. The relation between tradition and orthodoxy in the past is evident enough.[15]

In the light of the tract, Thomas' sermon in *Murder in the Cathedral* takes on some relevance. But whether Thomas —or Eliot—expects his audience to appreciate this state of mind of his is doubtful. Thomas admits:

> What yet remains to show of my history
> Will seem to most of you at best futility,
> Senseless self-slaughter of a lunatic,
> Arrogant passion of a fanatic.

Should this mystical revelation be missed by anyone, Eliot reiterates clearly enough throughout the whole play his contempt for life. Although the philosophy of *Murder in the Cathedral* treats of the superior soul in the twelfth century, Eliot means his message for his contemporaries. The Knights, for example, speak to a modern audience which has "now arrived at a just subordination of the pretensions of the .Church to the welfare of the State"; the Tempters refer to fireworks amd prizes for English essays; the chorus (acknowledging "ourselves as type of the common man") urges limited standards and acceptance of what comes:

> But we are content if we are left alone. . . .
> For us, the poor, there is no action,
> But only to wait and to witness.

Progress is likely to be difficult:

> Men learn little from others' experience.
> But in the life of one man, never
> The same time returns.

In any case, our lives are predestined: "Destiny waits in the hand of God, shaping the still unshapen"; and Thomas adds his comment to that of the chorus: "All things prepare the event."

Except for its novelty, which drew audiences seeking a new titillation, *Murder in the Cathedral* is poor theatre. A vague, ill-defined impression of some religious feeling, apparently experienced by the main character, is not made intelligible to the other characters or to the audience. Yet in some ways, the lack of explanation here is not quite as

crippling as it is in the later plays. The audience for whom
the play was originally written were Anglicans who would
have some sympathy with the historical situation, just as a
Greek audience would have sympathy for and knowledge
of the stories retold by Aeschylus; and the mood pictures
Eliot gives the verse-speaking chorus can be enjoyed quite
independently of the play.

A still better example of what happens when literature is
harnessed to plough a theological furrow already traced
out occurs in *The Family Reunion*—"Mr. Eliot's worst
failure," as his admirer, Miss Muriel C. Bradbrook called
it;[16] "a masterpiece" according to Mr. E. Martin Browne.[17]
The formula which Eliot adopts for *The Family Reunion*
is found in his essay *After Strange Gods,* where Eliot expands on one of his basic credos, the idea of Original Sin:

> At this point I shall venture to generalise, and suggest
> that with the disappearance of the idea of Original
> Sin, with the disappearance of the idea of intense
> moral struggle, the human beings presented to us both
> in poetry and in prose fiction to-day, and more pat-
> ently among the serious writers than in the under-
> world of letters, tend to become less and less real. It is
> in fact in moments of moral and spiritual struggle de-
> pending upon spiritual sanctions, rather than in those
> 'bewildering minutes' in which we are all very much
> alike, that men and women come nearest to being real.
> If you do away with this struggle, and maintain that
> by tolerance, benevolence, inoffensiveness and a re-
> distribution or increase of purchasing power, com-
> bined with a devotion, on the part of an élite, to Art,
> the world will be as good as anyone could require,

then you must expect human beings to become more
and more vaporous.[18]

Eliot's problem is to make the concept of original sin acceptable to a modern audience, and he hopes that by writing
to this prescription he will make his characters become more
and more real. We may believe that Eliot had in mind a sim-
iliar attempt in *Sweeney Agonistes,* although the brief
snatches which made up the tiny volume need considerable
elucidation, because he tried, in a highly artificial way, to
attract an audience by superimposing jazz, music hall, and
melodramatic idioms on a theological substructure. In
Sweeney Agonistes Eliot worked on the same themes he
was to employ in *The Family Reunion* and in *The Cocktail
Party* as well—guilt feelings, the sense of sin, the need to
atone, and how these feelings may be absolved. The two
epigraphs heading *Sweeney Agonistes* summarize all three
plays:

> Orestes: You don't see them, you don't—but *I* see
> them: they are hunting me down, I must move
> on.—*Choephoroi.*

> Hence the soul cannot be possessed of the divine
> union, until it has divested itself of the love of cre-
> ated beings.—St. John of the Cross.

Indeed, the first quotation is incorporated into the text of
The Family Reunion (page 24), and the second is incorporated in spirit many times in *The Cocktail Party,* for
example, in Reilly's "Let me free your mind from one im-
pediment: You must try to detach yourself from what you
still feel As your responsibility." Or in Celia's "a revela-

tion about my relationship with *everybody*. Do you know
—It no longer seems worth while to *speak* to anyone!"

The Orestes theme, like that of Oedipus, has attracted
other twentieth-century playwrights trying to explain a
"curse." Eliot once referred to the "kind of pattern which
we perceive in our own lives only at rare moments of inat-
tention and detachment, drowsing in sunlight. It is the pattern drawn by what the ancient world called Fate; subtil-
ized by Christianity into mazes of delicate theology; and
reduced again by the modern world into crudities of psychological or economic necessity." [19] O'Neill has retold the
whole story in terms of late nineteenth-century New England, and has so transferred the "pattern" that *Mourning
Becomes Electra,* no matter what its merits as a stage play
may be, is understandable by contemporary standards of
conduct. In *Les Mouches* (The Flies) Sartre stresses, along
with what he considers the psychological needs for group
guilt, the political necessities of the legend.

But for Eliot the main interest is not mythological or psychological but religious. He selected the Orestes story, particularly in *The Family Reunion,* not only because it could
be made to fit a doctrine of original sin, but because in the
Orestes legend salvation or the removal of guilt came about
through the intervention of the gods. The effects here are
further Christianized by leaving the actual crime in doubt.
It is never made clear whether Harry had really murdered
his wife; the implication is that the thought is the same as
the deed.

Both *The Family Reunion* and *The Cocktail Party* have a
similar theme: the application of religious rules to the dif-

ficulties of individuals in the modern world; or, to put it in Eliot's terms, how one can be cured of a sense of sin. In this aspect, Harry, the protagonist of *The Family Reunion,* with his feelings of aloneness and of guilt, resembles Celia of *The Cocktail Party.* The "solution" to Harry's problem is similarly undertaken by a character who only later reveals herself to be like Celia's Doctor Reilly, somebody who is more than natural, a spokesman for the gods.

The plot of *The Family Reunion* concerns the "curing" of the murder fixation of a young nobleman, Harry, Lord Monchensey. Having wished his wife dead, Harry imagines that he has, "that cloudless night in the mid-Atlantic," pushed his wife overboard from the deck of a liner. Harry had been brought up in complete subjugation to his mother (the father having left her when Harry was still a child). When he grew up, his rebellion against this maternal yoke drove him into a defiant marriage. But the hasty union was not successful, and the hostility he had borne his mother was transferred to his wife. His chauffeur-valet, describing the night when Lady Monchensey was drowned, reveals how Harry's conscious mind was battling with the subconscious wish:

> I mean to say, you could see that he was nervous.
> He behaved as if he thought something might happen. . . .
> But he seemed very anxious about my Lady.
> Tried to keep her in when the weather was rough,
> Didn't like to see her lean over the rail.

During the succeeding year, Harry became plagued with the thought that he murdered his wife—*or* may have murdered her! "Perhaps I only dreamt I pushed her." His brain is filled with the memories of these events, so that he can find no peace of mind:

> When I remember them
> They leave me alone: when I forget them
> Only for an instant of inattention
> They are roused again, the sleepless hunters
> That will not let me sleep.

In an effort to escape from these anxieties, he returns to his ancestral home, Wishwood, but his disturbance is aggravated by the memories of his unhappy childhood:

> It seems I shall get rid of nothing,
> Of none of the shadows that I wanted to escape;
> And at the same time, other memories,
> Earlier, forgotten, begin to return
> Out of my childhood.

Although Eliot includes a country physician in the cast, the part of "healer" is played by an aunt, "the efficient principal of a women's college" at Oxford. How efficient she would be is an open question. Miss Helen Gardner, herself an Oxford don, has this comment on the characterization of Aunt Agatha: "it is difficult to believe in the efficiency if she really had to spend as much of her energy as she suggests in 'trying not to dislike women.' I cannot imagine any body of Fellows in the world consenting to her election as Principal." [20]

Aunt Agatha explains to Harry (inspired to ask questions by a remark dropped by the physician) that his father had no love for his mother, but sired her three sons and then went away. One day,

> I found him thinking
> How to get rid of your mother. . . .
> You were due in three months
> time;
> You could not have been born in that event: I
> stopped him.

Harry apparently sees that his own antipathy toward his wife was not due to his own character or to circumstances which he could have controlled, but followed inevitably from his upbringing. He realizes that this mother's love was all-enveloping and extended so far as to strangle his love for a wife, and that he has transferred the animosity from his mother to his wife. His guilt, therefore, is less in himself and more in the environing background. Understanding the reasons why his father left his mother, understanding now his mother's warped hatred against any girl who would deprive her of her son, understanding her bitter feud for thirty years with her sister Agatha who she feels stole her husband's affections, understanding too his own substitution of wife for mother, and his loveless childhood, Harry is able to place his feelings for his wife in their proper pattern, and to begin to disconnect his hatred from his wife's drowning. Some of his terrible feeling of inner guilt is removed.

At this point, Eliot decides to give a supernatural account of Harry's relief. At the end of his expression of happiness that he is freed from his oppression, Harry says:

> Look, I do not know why,
> I feel happy for a moment, as if I had come home.
> It is quite irrational, but now
> I feel quite happy, as if happiness
> Did not consist in getting what one wanted
> Or in getting rid of what can't be got rid of
> But in a different vision. This is like an end.

To his "This is like an end," Agatha adds mystically (foreshadowing the *Four Quartets*), "And a beginning"; and a little later prophesies "You have a long journey." Harry comments:

> I know that I have made a decision
> In a moment of clarity, and now I feel dull again.
> I only know that I made a decision
> Which your words echo. I am still befouled,
> But I know there is only one way out of defile-
>   ment—
> Which leads in the end to reconciliation.
> And I know that I must go.

To the entreaties of his mother that he stay, he says:

> Only be sure
> That I know what I am doing, and what I must do,
> And that it is the best thing for everybody.
> But at present, I cannot explain it to anyone:
> I do not know the words in which to explain it—
> That is what makes it harder. You must just believe
>   me,
> Until I come again.

Eliot had hoped, through thus dramatizing his idea of original sin, to give his characters greater reality; but his characters remain lifeless. One of his favorable critics has said that the most real characters are the two brothers who are talked about but never appear in the play! Certainly Harry, the protagonist, is only two-dimensional. Nowhere does he come to life. There is no development of character. The Eumenides influence Harry's thoughts and actions, but they are not the personifications of his feelings of guilt, his "origin of wretchedness," because others see and discuss them. They are objective.[21] (Shakespeare knew better when he made Banquo's ghost invisible to all save his murderer. Eliot's Eumenides are about as apt as a dagger suspended by a string from the proscenium arch in a performance of *Macbeth*.)

Although Harry makes a decision in the course of the play, determined to face rather than flee this "ring of ghosts with joined hands," he remains the same when he leaves as when he enters. If an author decides not to show development—a difficult decision especially in plays where character change is the chief dramatic resource—he must as the only alternative show an increasing depth of characterization: if he does neither, his characters will be but mouthpieces. Eliot's characters are just that. Harry can give no explanation for his decision, just as Celia in *The Cocktail Party* can give no reasons for her decision to become a nun.

Harry's fears and inability to face life go deeper than his fear of having killed his wife, but after some explanation of him family background, Harry's comment is:

> I only now begin to have some understanding
> Of you, and of all of us.

Two pages later, however, Harry has a sudden moment of happiness, or "a different vision." He says he has "made a decision In a moment of clarity." The audience is never told, even in symbols or allusions, what this "moment of clarity" consists of, and why Harry is going away.

Harry is not an individual: he is a type manufactured to represent what Eliot wants him to represent. Harry is an earlier Celia, and suffers from the same complaints. In *The Cocktail Party* Celia describes her two worries, the "two things I can't understand, which you might consider symptoms," namely,

> An awareness of solitude. . . .
> . . . what has happened has made me aware
> That I've always been alone. . . .

and, secondly, "a sense of sin." In a long speech, Harry enumerates these same symptoms—the isolation of the individual:

> At the beginning, eight years ago,
> I felt, at first, that sense of separation,
> Of isolation unredeemable, irrevocable—
> It's eternal, or gives a knowledge of eternity,
> Because it feels eternal while it lasts. That is one
>   hell. . . .

and the sense of sin—here, of course, of a crime which he persuades himself he is really guilty of:

> And then I had no horror of my action,
> I only felt the repetition of it
> Over and over. . . .

> Here I have been finding
> A misery long forgotten, and a new torture,
> The shadow of something behind our meagre
>   childhood,
> Some origin of wretchedness.

Apart from the speeches where he makes direct reference to the Eumenides, Harry's lines could just as well be given to Celia. Here is Harry (1939):

> The things I thought were real are shadows, and
>   the real
> Are what I thought were private shadows.

And Celia (1950):

> I don't hear any voices, I have no delusions—
> Except that the world I live in seems all a delu-
>   sion. . . .

and

> It must be some kind of hallucination;
> Yet, at the same time, I'm frightened by the fear
> That it is more real than anything I believed in.

Is not Harry's speech an earlier version of Celia's:

> A dream. I was happy in it till today. . . .
> Perhaps the dream was better. It seemed the real
>   reality,
> And if this is reality, it is very like a dream.

Harry gives the longest statement of unworldliness in a speech which without change would fit Celia in the later play:

> What you call the normal
> Is merely the unreal and the unimportant.
> I was like that in a way, so long as I could think
> Even of my own life as an isolated ruin,
> A casual bit of waste in an orderly universe.
> But it begins to seem just part of some huge dis-
>   aster,
> Some monstrous mistake and aberration
> Of all men, of the world, which I cannot put in
>   order.

Harry, as a hero, is less attractive than Celia, though dramatically his problem (the fact that a woman has died, and in some way he was involved) is more intelligible. He is mentally sick, and far more in need of the ministrations of a psychiatrist than is Celia. The pattern of an Orestes complex is obvious enough to the patient himself, so that, learning of his father's hostility to his mother, Harry discards his feelings of imagined guilt. The mystical explanation is superfluous, and is introduced only to satisfy Eliot's religiosity.

The immediate reaction of the rest of his family to Harry's decision that

> I have my course to pursue, and I am safe from
>   normal dangers
> If I pursue it. I cannot account for this
> But it is so, mother. Until I come again. . . .

is given by Amy: "Harry is going away—to become a missionary." Harry neither confirms nor denies this statement; all he says is, "I never said that I was going to be a missionary." But again the implication is that he is entering upon some stage of religious exercises which will take him away from the world as we know it.

The need to spread his beliefs makes Eliot sprinkle his play with crudely dogmatic statements. The audience gets a sermon: suffering is good. "To rest in our own suffering Is evasion of suffering. We must learn to suffer more." This is the verse equivalent of his program of education given in *Thoughts after Lambeth*: "Thought, study, mortification, sacrifice: it is such notions as these that should be impressed upon the young." [22] Or his dismissal of the horrors of war: "Yet I have no more sympathy with the purely humanitarian attitude toward war than with the humanitarian attitude toward anything else: I should not enjoy the prospect of abolishing suffering without at the same time perfecting human nature." [23]

In identical terms to *The Cocktail Party* a man is told that all he can expect in life is

> the transparent deception
> The keeping up of appearances
> The making the best of a bad job. . . .
> There is nothing at all to be done about it.
> There is nothing to do about anything.

Lest the message of supra-rationalism be missed, the limitations of the mind are explicitly affirmed in *The Family Reunion*:

> Except for a limited number
> Of strictly practical purposes
> We do not know what we are doing;

And even, when you think about it,
We do not know much about thinking.

These opinions are dogmatically stated either by Agatha or the Chorus; there is no doubt of their emphasis. The
main philosophical direction of *The Family Renunion*
is anti-worldly; echoes of Plato and St. Paul mingle happily
together:

You have gone through life in sleep,
Never woken to the nightmare. I tell you, life
would be unendurable
If you were wide awake.

Throughout the play, predestination is accepted. With
Edward's lines in *The Cocktail Party,* "I see that my life
was determined long ago," we can compare Harry's

O God, man, the things that are going to happen
Have already happened. . . .

along with the whole elaborate build-up of the theory "all
past is present" (p. 29) and "everything is irrevocable The
past unredeemable," two phrases repeated from "Burnt
Norton":

Time present and time past
Are both perhaps present in time future,
And time future contained in time past.
If all time is eternally present
All time is unredeemable.

In *The Family Reunion* the intrusion of dogma, the writing to illustrate a thesis, have killed the drama. The critics
have devoted little attention to this play perhaps because it

is so bad, and perhaps because they wish to ignore the reasons why it is bad. Stephen Spender, however, also a poet and dramatist, has voiced his opinions, and with them we may leave *The Family Reunion*: "Eliot's plays have suffered in the past from a certain self-conscious forcing of the moral pace to underline the 'message' of the play, as though he did not feel confident that he could create a situation from which this would arise." And again: "The plots were weak because the purpose of the chief character in *Murder in the Cathedral* and *The Family Reunion* was to impose a moral on the audience." [24]

The faults of *The Family Reunion* recur in Eliot's latest and more successful play, *The Cocktail Party*. One of its drawbacks is that Celia, who is far more interesting than the ever-present Chamberlaynes, appears very little. Her great crisis, when she decides to devote herself to the religious life, occupies a slim fourteen pages of text. There is no change in, or indeed any illumination on, her emotions or her character at this time. Here is a valid problem for a writer: what goes on in the mind of an intelligent and sensitive young woman, dissatisfied with her twentieth-century cocktail society, who is persuaded to enter a nunnery? All we get from Eliot is:

> I don't in the least know what I'm doing
> Or why I am doing it.

Celia's conversion, although the core, is actually the most unsatisfactory part of *The Cocktail Party*. At the end of Act I (Scene 3), she has decided to go away from the vapid people with whom she has been associating, a not unexpected decision in view of the break with Edward and the impending departure of Peter. Several times she is on the point of explaining her feelings following this shock, but someone or something interrupts. In her talk with Edward, Celia says, "And I ask you to forgive me." Edward: "You . . . ask me to forgive *you!*" Celia: "Yes, for two things. First. . . ." Then *"The telephone rings."* We never know what the two things are. A little later, Edward is uttering his refrain:

> I wish I could, I wish I understood anything,
> I'm completely in the dark.

Celia tells him: "But it's all so simple. Can't you see that. . . ." This time, *"The doorbell rings."* Thus Eliot avoids the difficulty of an explanation. This period in Celia's life is important, because it is the only time during her appearances on the stage that the audience can be prepared for her decision, "several weeks later," to enter a nunnery. Celia appears next in the consulting-room of Harcourt-Reilly (pp. 130-145). She describes the obvious reactions of a girl having been "ditched," and then starts talking of "sin" and "atonement." These terms should be at least partially explained: Celia defines sin negatively—it is not a feeling of immorality, but "some kind of hallucination"—and ignores the second word. She merely tells us:

> I want to be cured
> Of a craving for something I cannot find
> And of the shame of never finding it.

Reilly exploits her confusion to prescribe her "going away." For the crisis in her life, and for the part this crisis plays in the whole play, these fourteen pages are quite inadequate. Her groping descriptions and vague terminology give no penetration in depth—if her character is static, and Eliot is studying a person frozen at a turning point in her life. Nor is there any development: Celia is the same girl flirting with Edward, turning from him, and discussing her desertion with Reilly. All we see is a bewildered woman accepting without reason the dictatorial prescription of a medicine man. And what happens to her afterwards, during those two years when she assumedly was working out her "salvation with diligence," and which enabled her to have a "happy" death, is not even hinted at.

Just as the poetry and drama are confused, so is Eliot's prose. Here, the whirligig of double-talk unbalances the reader and totters him into propaganda. In his devotion to theory, Eliot ignores logic, surrenders the intellect to prejudice, and imposes his own views and practices, whether they fit or not, on history and literature.

In his overall literary criticism Eliot has set out to reinterpret literary history and literature. It is true that every age has its own approach to writings of the past, and Eliot has noted that, "From time to time, every hundred years or so, it is desirable that some critic shall appear to review the past of our literature, and set the poets and the poems in a new order." [25] In so doing, Eliot has demonstrated what his new order consists of. It is to deny progressive values won in the struggles of the last three or four hundred years. His course would divert English letters into a by-channel. In his "review," Eliot exalts writers who have opposed progress, or any change, and belittles and passes over those who have supported humanism. The evidence is clear that Eliot's religious and political conservatism prejudices his views on certain writers.

His hostility to Milton, which continues despite the 1947 British Academy lecture where he apparently switches sides,[26] is startling. Significant is his selection of seventeenth-century writers. Perhaps because of his attitude toward modern society, Eliot was attracted to the seventeenth century, the greatest period of literary production of the rising mercantile classes. Yet Eliot was attracted not by the virile and progressive writers, but by those already showing decadent elements. His heroes are Webster ("the last ripeness" of the Elizabethans) and Crashaw. On the other hand, Eliot has scarcely a good word to say for the liberal minds, for Milton, for Bacon, for Bunyan, for Hobbes. Milton, he says, lacks "visual imagination," and his sensuousness has been "withered early by book-learning." [27] Eliot selects Marvell as speaking "more clearly and unequivocally with the voice of his literary age than does Milton." [28] Does Eliot object to Milton's liberal theology, which he says, "I find in large part repellent"? [29] Bacon is dismissed in two words for his "heavy sententiousness." [30] Eliot's passion against Hobbes is understandable, for Hobbes was the harbinger of the modern world, with his opposition to scholastic ideas and to the shams of medieval religion. An "extraordinary little upstart[s] " [31] is Eliot's judgment on the author of *Leviathan!*

Eliot carries his prejudices into later centuries. Burns becomes a "decadent representative of a great alien tradition" [32]—"decadent" perhaps because he wrote of men's equality? Of Shelley, Eliot writes, "I find his ideas repellent," [33] and his beliefs "excite my abhorrence." [34] Of later writers, Dickens is merely a "decadent genius";[35] the "individualistic morals" of George Eliot are to be deplored;[36] "the large part" of Whitman's content is "claptrap";[37] Hardy was "indifferent even to the prescripts of good writing";[38] Wells "lapses from vulgarity into high seriousness";[39] Shaw "reveals himself as the artist whose development was checked at puberty." [40]

Eliot's idiosyncratic interpretation of English literature, his sneers at the humanist traditions, suggest the reasons for his inability to rise above the achievement of his early years, and explain his subsequent deterioration as poet and critic. Eliot has himself remarked the self-revelation that often accompanies one poet's criticism of another: "For poets, when they meditate about poetry at all, are liable to generalize either from their own accomplishment or from their own designs; and their purposes and interests, if more exact, may also be narrower than those of their readers, so that their pronouncements should usually be considered in relation to their own poems." [41]

It is a curious coincidence that, in his criticism of these authors, Eliot ascribes his own weaknesses to them. Thus his verse is to some extent withered by book learning; his drama exhibits heavy sententiousness (as Eliot has admitted of his prose); his philosophy for many excites abhorrence; and his artistic development seems to have been arrested at puberty (I have noted the adolescent pornography of *"Dans le Restaurant"* used for the core Section IV of *The Waste Land*). Sometimes a weakness is exalted into a virtue. Eliot has gone to great lengths to resuscitate Dryden, "one other great writer who put politics into verse." [42]

The devotion to a rigid philosophy, with attendant neglect of the world, is a convenient alibi for Eliot's avoidance of decisions. We find it in *The Idea of a Christian Society,* despite the concern, expressed in his preface, with "a direction of religious thought which must inevitably proceed to a criticism of political and economic systems." [43] But Eliot wriggles away from this "direction" and out of a conclusion: "In ignoring these problems, I am not taking refuge in a mere admission of incompetence, though the suspicion that I am incompetent might operate against the acceptance of any observations that I made; nor am I simply resigning them to the supposed technical authorities, for that would be a surrender to the primacy of ethics." He continues: "My point is that, while there is a considerable measure of agreement that certain things are wrong, the question of how they should be put right is so extremely controversial, that any proposal is immediately countered by a dozen others; and in this context, attention would be concentrated on the imperfections of my proposals, and away from my main concern, the end to be attained." [44]

Eliot's criticism is destructive and, where it attempts to be positive, so vague (avoiding the controversial) as to have little meaning. In point of fact, in this particular essay, his "end to be attained" is possibly more controversial than any suggestions for putting things right could ever be.

At other times Eliot simply ignores the conclusion to which his argument must lead, when it is at variance with his special religious views. I have already given an example of this wide-awake blindness—his disregard for the positive values of the French Revolution and the American Civil War (pp. 9-12), each of which was, whatever distress and dislocation they caused their countries, the only means for destroying certain evils. Revolutions cannot be condoned easily; but entrenched tyrannies cannot be condoned at all. Again, (p. 38), Eliot ignores the economic basis of imperialism and fascism, although he admits the "hypertrophy of the Profit motive" in his own society. But Italy and Germany supplied more than enough evidence that their fascism was the consequence of something more than the lack of a functioning religion. Such a theory would not fit in with his claims for the supremacy of religion, and so it is not even considered.

Another instance is Eliot's refusal to discuss whether the Reformation from the point of view of cultural activity was "a good or a bad thing" (p. 53). Were the question so framed, Eliot's theory that separation from Rome represented for England "a diversion from the main stream of culture" would be untenable in view of the notable advance in range and quality of English culture after 1550.

We have another such evasion in *The Cocktail Party,* where Reilly presents the choice of two ways for Celia, realizing that she has good will and energy to work for a cause. He shows the way of the Chamberlaynes, a dull, routine acceptance of the shortcomings of life. The other way is that of complete surrender to a supernatural cause. This is a deception because there is a third choice: that Celia strive together with others to free the world from that dullness and boredom which is the lot of the Chamberlaynes.

A similar unwarranted restriction of choice occurs in the *Notes towards the Definition of Culture*:

> It is commonly assumed that there is culture, but that it is the property of a small section of society; and from this assumption it is usual to proceed to one of two conclusions: either that culture can only be the concern of a small minority, and that therefore there is no place for it in the society of the future; or that in the society of the future the culture which has been the possession of the few must be put at the disposal of everybody.[45]

By 1949 it should have been obvious that in the society of the future, the culture will not be identical with ours, but will be that of the *new* society, whatever it is; there is not the slightest reason to suggest that it can only be the culture of everybody or else the culture of nobody.

One final instance of Eliot's avoidance or neglect of conclusions which would lead him into difficulties comes in *The Idea of a Christian Society*:

> But I believe that if these countries [the United States and the Dominions] are to develop a positive culture of their own, and not remain merely derivatives of Europe, they can only proceed either in the direction of a pagan or of a Christian society. I am not suggesting that the latter alternative must lead to the forcible suppression, or to the complete disappearance of dissident sects; still less, I hope, to a superficial union of Churches under an official exterior, a union in which theological differences would be so belittled that its Christianity might become wholly bogus. But a positive culture must have a positive set of values, and the

dissentients must remain marginal, tending to make
only marginal contributions.[46]

This passage is misleading for a number of reasons. In the
first place Eliot ignores the fact that India, a Dominion of
the British Commonwealth, possesses an indigenous culture. If we agree with Eliot that this is a non-Christian culture, and therefore pagan, we should point out that India
had a positive culture of its own at the time Eliot was writing: there is no question of India *developing* a culture.
Eliot assumes that the culture will be Christian; what kind
of Christian he does not say; and he avoids any suggestion
as to the kind of Christian society he envisages for the
United States. But the conclusion he sidetracks is the un-
pleasant one he mentions in *After Strange Gods,* which
has here become: those outside the brand of Christianity
that Eliot decides has a "positive set of values" become
"marginal." How are these dissentients to be persuaded that
their religion or culture is marginal? How is this process to
be achieved without "forcible suppression"? To admit that
"forcible suppression" is probably the only way would be
to emphasize Eliot's position that "a spirit of excessive tolerance is to be deprecated." [47]

There is actually very little in Eliot's later essays (predominantly moralistic, not literary) to qualify him as an
original or profound thinker. Indeed, there is much that is
banal; his opinion of war, for example, if written by anyone
without his reputation, would be laughed out of existence:
"I think that no one can doubt that war in the form in
which we have known it in our time, while it gives a few affirmed Christians the opportunity to realize their virtues in

action—whether in submission or in protest—and while it often brings out amazing natural virtues, is on the whole degrading." [48] In his most recent critical work, the *Notes,* there is a remarkable statement: "Every change we make is tending to bring about a new civilization of the nature of which we are ignorant, and in which we should all of us be unhappy." [49] It is hard to lend any meaning to this pronouncement. How is it possible to have an opinion of something the nature of which is unknown?

Examples of such slovenly thinking increase in his later works, while the clever phrase and the concrete example diminish. Eliot's way of life was ready-made, although he may have struggled to make it his own. Because of his unconditional acceptance, it became a strait jacket which prevented his mind from ranging where it would and coming to logical conclusions. The prime example is the *Notes towards the Definition of Culture.* Every chapter could be shown to be woolly and confused. A valuable short article debunking much of this book has appeared in the Cambridge quarterly, *Scrutiny.* In addition to pointing out specific obscurities, the author gives the overall objection that Eliot

> seems to show no consciousness of many important factors which are having a visible effect on culture today. He neglects the inevitable impact of material, especially of economic, forces on society. . . . Similarly, he shows no recognition of the great changes in the form of wealth which are basically modifying the relations of classes to each other. To put the point unkindly for the moment, as far as Eliot is concerned,

[F. R. Leavis'] *Culture and Environment* might never have been written.[50]

Notes towards the Definition of Culture carries an Appendix of broadcasts to Germany entitled "The Unity of European Culture." This contains a paragraph (on p. 126) which may serve to illustrate the slovenly and confused thinking to which Eliot has sunk. Let us analyze it, sentence by sentence.

1. *The dominant force in creating a common culture between two peoples each of which has its distinct culture, is religion.*

Eliot is speaking of "certain common features in Europe which make it possible to speak of a European culture" (end of preceding paragraph, p. 125). What does Eliot include in this "European" culture? He has nowhere in this talk excluded Eastern Europe which has never accepted Latin traditions, although elsewhere (p. 74) he talks of a Roman or Latin tradition for the Western world (by which he means the Western *European* world). He is here discussing, actually, not European culture, but *Western* European culture. But the whole sentence is circular. Eliot says (p. 73): "The formation of a religion is also the formation of a culture." Consequently, the distinct cultures are formed by the same religion which is going to be the dominant force in creating a common culture.

2. *Please do not, at this point, make a mistake in anticipating my meaning.*

3. *This is not a religious talk, and I am not setting out to convert anybody.*

Not so advertised, no doubt. But essentially religious, be-

cause, not dealing with facts (see 4 below) but with interpretation, the talk is angled to emphasize the importance of
religion for culture.

4. *I am simply stating a fact.*

For "fact" read "my interpretation of history." See comments below for historical inaccuracies.

5. *I am not so much concerned with the communion of
Christian believers today; I am talking about the common
tradition of Christianity which has made Europe what it is,
and about the common cultural elements which this common Christianity has brought with it.*

Christianity today is divided; and "we are prepared to
find that the division between Christian cultures will stimu-
late further differentiations of belief and cult" (p. 73). England, at the time of the Reformation, diverged "from the
main stream of culture." Eliot, therefore, is going back to
before the Reformation, to the Middle Ages, when, for
four or five hundred years there was some kind of "common tradition" and "common cultural elements." His
Christianity is here limited to medieval Catholicism, but by
implication, this is what he accepts as modern twentieth-
century Christianity (See 11, 13 below).

6. *If Asia were converted to Christianity tomorrow, it
would not thereby become a part of Europe.*

Sentence 1 (above) states that a common culture is created from two distinct cultures by religion. Asia has a "distinct culture"; why then should not a common culture be
created from it and a European "distinct culture," if each
has the same religion? In that case, Asia would be "a part
of Europe" culturally.

7. *It is in Christianity that our arts have developed; it is in Christianity that the laws of Europe have—until recently —been rooted.*

True, for about 1100 to 1500; if by "developed" we mean that the Church was the patron of the arts, having the money to pay the craftsmen. As soon as other social organizations developed which had the money to sponsor art, the importance of the Church as sponsor of the arts waned— *e.g.,* rich Dutch merchants and their commissioning of secular portraits and tapestries, markets and guildhalls, etc. Eliot omits mention of the parts played by Greece and Rome in the development of arts. The statement is historically true for only a few hundred years, and it throws no light on the development of the arts in other periods.

The second part of the sentence is false: for at least five or six centuries Christianity was struggling to survive, and in no position to make laws. The tradition of Western law is rooted in pagan Rome, and (for common law in England and hence in parts of America) in pre-Christian pagan regulations. Only in a few instances, such as the medieval prohibition against usury and restrictions against Jews, was Christianity the positive influence, and such laws no longer hold. Eliot is vague about "until recently." Does he mean the Reformation, or does he refer to Russia? If the latter, was Orthodox Russia in the common culture of Western Europe (cf. p. 94, "The oriental cast of the Russian mind")?

8. *It is against a background of Christianity that all our thought has significance.*

What does "thought" mean? The sentence may be true only if we mean philosophic thought. It is difficult to see what significance Christianity can give to scientific thought: it may give significance to the *use* made of scientific thought.

9. *An individual European may not believe that the Christian Faith is true, and yet what he says, and makes, and does, will all spring out of his heritage of Christian culture and depend upon that culture for its meaning.*

Eliot refutes this sentence earlier in his book (p. 73). "The result of the unquestioned dominance of one cult, when a people is passive, may be torpor: when a people is quick and self-assertive, the result may be chaos. For, as discontent turns to disaffection, the anti-clerical bias may become an anti-religious tradition; *a distinct and hostile culture grows and flourishes,* and a nation is divided against itself." But Eliot proved that we have no Christian culture now, and that "the culture has become secularised," that "the boundary between belief and unbelief is vague," and that Christians and atheists live in amity "so long as they continue to accept some common moral conventions."

10. *Only a Christian culture could have produced a Voltaire or a Nietzche.*

True in the sense that all men are conditioned by the society into which they were born, and if Voltaire and Nietzsche were born into societies which were mainly Christian (since Eliot equates religion with culture), then it is true that only a Christian society could produce anti-Christians. But then how about such anti-Christians as Islam? Or does Eliot mean only Christian anti-Christians?

11. *I do not believe that the culture of Europe could survive the complete disappearance of the Christian Faith.*

See 13 below, and compare Eliot's own words (p. 71):
"On the other hand, we must acknowledge that many of the
most remarkable achievements of culture have been made
since the sixteenth century, in conditions of disunity; and
that some, indeed, as in nineteenth-century France, appear
after the religious foundations for culture seem to have
crumbled away. We cannot affirm that if the religious unity
of Europe had continued, these or equally brilliant achievements would have been realised. Either religious unity or
religious division may coincide with cultural efflorescence
or cultural decay."

12. *And I am convinced of that, not merely because I
am a Christian myself, but as a student of social biology.*
What is "social biology"? An Eliotism for "sociology"?
(Cf. p. 69: "I attempt, as far as possible, to contemplate my
problems from the point of view of the sociologist.") Or
something much more sinister: biologism, treating human
beings as animals?

13. *If Christianity goes, the whole of our culture goes.*
What does Eliot mean by "Christianity"? All the faiths
and sects taken together? The Catholic churches? The
Church of England? The Roman Catholic Church? The
Orthodox Church? The Protestant groups? As far as England is concerned, the Roman Church has "gone," yet England still has "culture"; and in France, Eliot has admitted
that the Roman Church (Christianity in France) has gone,
yet there have been still "some of the most remarkable
achievements of culture" (p. 71). And what does "our culture" signify? Eliot in the following paragraph includes
"the literatures of Greece and Rome," "the ancient civilisa-

tions of Greece, Rome and Israel." Eliot's European culture, therefore, was flourishing long before the advent of Christianity.

14. *Then you must start painfully again, and you cannot put on a new culture ready made.*

See 16 below.

15. *You must wait for the grass to grow to feed the sheep to give the wool out of which your new coat will be made.*

16. *You must pass through many centuries of barbarism.*

This may have been true of the development of a Christian culture. Since man's development has become more and more rapid (*e.g.*, the last 400 years have seen more changes and advances than the previous 4,000), there is no reason to assume many centuries of "barbarism" before any new culture develops. The sentence exaggerates the length and depth of the actual period of decline; and at any rate is a hackneyed and nonscholarly picture of the dark ages.

17. *We should not live to see the new culture, nor would our great-great-great-grand-children: and if we did, not one of us would be happy in it.*

The Soviet Union and the Eastern European countries profess to be making a new non-Christian culture, and have already produced some results (*e.g.*, Russian music, films), whatever their merits. The latter part of the sentence is nonsense: if we shall not live to see the new culture, how do we know what it will be like? This is a repetition of "Every change we make is tending to bring about a new civilisation of the nature of which we are ignorant, and in which we should all of us be unhappy" (p. 16).

The compulsion of dogma colors the intellectual background of all of Eliot's writing. He seems to have followed a "line" and made his works conform to it. The "cloth" determines the suit. The dogma influences even the handling of words.

We are brought back to the most obvious feature of Eliot's overall philosophy, his contempt for people, and a corresponding contempt for communication. People are not worth bothering about; therefore it does not matter whether they understand what the artist has to say to them. When Eliot proclaims his concern as an author with his language, it is not with the intention of making clearer what he has to say to the majority of his potential reading public, but to cultivate a language so rarefied that only the initiates will understand.

In a passage from the little read *The New English Weekly* Eliot again stresses the importance of words: "A ceaseless care, a passionate and untiring devotion to language, is the first conscious concern of the poet; it demands a study of how his language has been written, in both prose and verse, in the past, and sensitiveness to the merits and shortcomings of the way in which it is spoken and written in his own time." [51] This statement in itself is not reactionary. It becomes so when taken in connection with his remarks in the earlier version of "The Social Function of Poetry": "We may say that the duty of the poet, as poet, is only indirectly to his people: his direct duty is to his *language,* first to preserve, and second to extend and improve." [52] But what is a language apart from the people who speak it and hear it?

Poetry and prose and drama to Eliot tend to become media of *un*-communication. Obscurity is a major defect of all his production.

Along with other prejudices of Eliot, the cult of obscurity is elevated into a critical dogma—meaning does not matter. In *The Use of Poetry,* Eliot says emphatically: "The more seasoned reader, he who has reached in these matters, a state of greater *purity*, does not bother about understanding; not, at least, at first." [53] Elsewhere he writes: "If the last two 'Quartets' seem obscure to some, then the obscurity there is inherent in the ideas expressed. . . . Finally, in the greatest works of art you never feel that you have reached a point where you understand everything." [54]

Again, in his introduction to Knight's *Wheel of Fire:*

> People ordinarily incline to suppose that in order to enjoy a poem it is necessary to "discover its meaning" so that their minds toil to discover a meaning, a meaning which they can expound to any one who will listen, in order to prove that they enjoy it. But for one thing, the possibilities of 'meaning' in poetry are so extensive, that one is quite aware that one's knowledge of the meaning even of what oneself has written is extremely limited, and that its meaning to others, at least so far as there is some consensus of interpretation among persons apparently qualified to interpret, is quite as much a part of it as what it means to oneself. [55]

In the earliest poetic drama, *Sweeney Agonistes,* there is no doubt about his indifference to conveying meaning in words:

> I gotta use words when I talk to you
> But if you understand or if you don't
> That's nothing to me and nothing to you.

Obscurity, remarkably enough, helped build up the legend of Eliot's artistry. On the one hand, it made critics hesitate to evaluate lines of whose meaning they were not too certain. Since attempts at interpretation would lay them open to other critics' possibly divergent views, most of them took the safer course of admitting the passages to be difficult or obscure. They went on to state that this difficulty or obscurity betokened great depth and significance. Thus the less the critics understood, the greater Eliot's writings became.

Amusing illustrations occur among the reviews of *The Cocktail Party*. For example, the Edinburgh *Scotsman* said, "It would be impossible to say exactly what is the philosophy which Mr. Eliot intends to express in this play," *but* it had "a lively entertainment face value," and "the wit sparkles." [56] The London *Daily Telegraph,* which admitted "it is true to some extent" that "the mind cannot grasp it," nevertheless claimed it as "one of the finest dramatic achievements of our time." [57] Alan Dent, in the London *News Chronicle,* noted this critical impasse, and was one of the few to dissent: "Some good critics have declared *The Cocktail Party* to be a fine play, but not one of them has told us straight out what it signifies. The week after—as well as the morning after—I take it to be nothing but a finely acted piece of flapdoodle." [58] This confession of bewilderment followed by acclaim was echoed by the American reviewers.

With more esoteric material, the practical results are in effect similar. On the concluding seven lines of the First Part of *The Waste Land,* at least three of the most serious Eliot critics took the plunge and emerged with three different interpretations. Yet the diversity of interpretation in this instance, just as the lack of it in the previous, is taken as a sign, not of a failure of the poet's technique, but, on the contrary, of his greatness. *Omne ignotum pro magnifico habetur.* So scholars, like the newspaper reviewers, mistake obscurity for profundity. The lines are well known:

'You who were with me in the ships at Mylae!
'That corpse you planted last year in your garden,
'Has it begun to sprout? Will it bloom this year?
'Or has the sudden frost disturbed its bed?
'Oh keep the Dog far hence, that's friend to men,
'Or with his nails he'll dig it up again!
'You! hypocrite lecteur!—mon semblable,—mon frère!'

The Dog is a symbol; but he is a troublesome, Protean animal. How shall he be interpreted? To Cleanth Brooks, the corpse is the buried Fertility God, and the Dog is "Humanitarianism and the related philosophies which, in their concern for man, extirpate the supernatural—dig up the corpse of the buried god and thus prevent the rebirth of life." [59] To Frank Wilson, the corpse is that of the hyacinth girl, which the Dog, "the traditional symbol of faithfulness," will root up out of the ground, like exposing a skeleton in a closet, and show "the faithlessness of modern marital relations." [60] Helen Gardner does not identify the corpse, but calls in the Bible to clarify the Dog:

The Psalmist's cry 'Deliver my soul from the sword, my darling from the power of the Dog' blends with a familiar image of a dog in a back-garden digging up, and bringing with friendly eagerness, to lay at his master's feet, something he had hoped he had disposed of. The feeling is very complex: we recoil in horror from the thought of the Dog, and in disgust from what the dog in the garden scratches up and brings us; but he is 'friend to men' perhaps even in his manifestation as the Dog, as much as when he lays at our feet some disgusting half-decayed object, wagging his tail with pleasure at his own cleverness.[61]

If three professors of English cannot agree on the symbolism of the Dog, what are ordinary readers to do?

Eliot had partly anticipated this question of divergent meanings in the W. P. Ker Memorial Lecture at the University of Glasgow in 1942. The premise is valid—that a reader has to re-create the poem for himself; but the implication seems questionable, that there can be no agreement among many readers what the poem is. Eliot makes a generalization that a reader's interpretation can be more valid than the author's, but elsewhere insists, in the case of *The Waste Land,* on his own interpretation, and gives the reader no latitude:

A poem may appear to mean very different things to different readers, and all of these meanings may be different from what the author thought he meant. For instance, the author may have been writing some peculiar personal experience, which he saw quite unrelated to anything outside; yet for the reader the poem may become the expression of a general situation, as well as some private experience of his own. The reader's interpretation may differ from the author's and be equally valid—it may even be better. There may be much more in a poem than the author was aware of.[62]

If he had recalled this passage, Nevill Coghill might have been less surprised that such divergency of interpretation is of no concern to Eliot. In the omnibus tribute compiled by Richard March and Tambimuttu, Coghill tells how he struggled with *Sweeney Agonistes* and that "he had got this far in fathoming the governing idea of these fragments—how impressive they now seemed—when a production of them was announced by Mr. Rupert Doone." [63] Doone, however, "offered an almost entirely different interpretation of the play to that I had worked out," namely, that all men are "Crippens" (or murderers) at heart. A year later, Coghill had lunch with Eliot and discussed this performance. He records the conversation in the following amusing way:[64]

> *Myself*: I had no idea the play meant what he [Mr. Doone] made of it . . . that everyone is a Crippen. I was astonished.
>
> *Mr Eliot*: So was I.
>
> *Myself*: Then you had meant something very different when you wrote it?
>
> *Mr Eliot*: Very different indeed.
>
> *Myself*: Yet you accept Mr. Doone's production?
>
> *Mr Eliot*: Certainly.
>
> *Myself*: But . . . but . . . can the play mean some-

> thing you didn't intend it to mean, you didn't
> know it meant?
> *Mr Eliot*: *Obviously it does.*
> *Myself*: But can it then also mean what you did
> intend?
> *Mr Eliot*: I hope so . . . yes, I think so.
> *Myself*: But if the two meanings are contradictory,
> is not one right and the other wrong? Must
> not the author be right?
> *Mr Eliot*: Not necessarily, do you think? Why is
> either wrong?

Obscurity in Eliot's verse is generally due to recondite references to earlier works of literature. Occasionally, recognition of these sources is not absolutely essential, although it may be desirable, for some enjoyment and comprehension of the poem. To appreciate such poems as "Portrait of a Lady" or "The Hippopotamus" it is not necessary to know that the former is an echo of Ezra Pound's *"Portraite d'une femme"* or the latter of Théophile Gautier's *"L'Hippopotame."* So too it is possible to derive some aesthetic satisfaction from, say, the stanza in "Whispers of Immortality":

> Grishkin is nice: her Russian eye
> Is underlined for emphasis;
> Uncorseted, her friendly bust
> Gives promise of pneumatic bliss. . . .

without knowing that it is, not a straight translation, but a parody of Gautier's lines from "Carmen":

> Carmen est maigre,—un trait de bistre
> Cerne son oeil de gitane,

Ses cheveux sont d'un noir sinistre
Sa peau, le diable la tanna.

There are few educated and cultured English-speaking
men and women sufficiently familiar with the course of
French poetry who could recognize this rather obscure
source and know the point of the parody. Still less could
a reader know the origin of a single line such as "simple
and faithless as a smile and shake of the hand" (*"La Figlia
Che Piange"*) from Laforgue's *"Simple et sans foi comme
un bonjour"* (*"Pétition"*). Or what well-educated man
could be expected to react spontaneously (without benefit
of gloss) to the out-of-the-way quotations in "Triumphal
March": to Husserl ("The natural wakeful life of our Ego
is a perceiving"), to Ludendorff (the catalogue of arma-
ments), or to Charles Maurras (*"Et les soldats faisaient la
haie? Ils la faisaient"*)? In all these examples, however, the
very fact that they are quotations or adaptations from other
writers must have some significance for the ideal reader—
to evoke some connotation at least. Otherwise why should
Eliot use the words of others? If the back reference is so
hidden, then the connotation cannot be made, and, even
though an interpretation of sorts is possible, some obscurity
is inevitable.

In time past, to a small group of readers with a uniform
education, including the minimum of Latin (and maybe
Greek), a poet's classical allusions could be expected to be
generally understood. There was a sufficiently homogeneous
audience for Milton's references not to seem artificial and
removed. Today, Milton has to be read with copious explanations. It is one of Eliot's criticisms of modern education

that it does not provide similarity of background. He believes a nation would be better "educated" if its people read fewer, but the same books. Thus, he claims, there might be some common ground for culture, in which a reference by a writer would be understood by his public: "You cannot expect continuity and coherence in literature and the arts, unless you have a certain uniformity of culture, expressed in education by a settled, though not rigid agreement as to what everyone should know to some degree, and a positive distinction—however undemocratic it may sound —between the educated and the uneducated." [65] As it is, he says, "our education indeed is so chaotic" that "you cannot make a quotation or an allusion to which the whole of any company can respond." [66]

Even when the quotations are recognizable or acknowledged, obscurity remains a danger. It may be noted, if the literary umbilical cords are in comparatively clear view, they can convey a variety of meanings fairly economically, as in the well-known lines from *The Waste Land*:

> But at my back from time to time I hear
> The sound of horns and motors, which shall bring
> Sweeny to Mrs Porter in the spring.

Here, an echo from Marvell's "To his Coy Mistress":

> But at my back I always hear
> Time's winged chariot hurrying near

is parodied and intermingled with words from "The Parliament of Bees," by another metaphysical poet, John Day:

When of the sudden, listening, you shall hear
A noise of horns and hunting, which shall bring
Actaeon to Diana in the spring
Where all shall see her naked skin.

Eliot has achieved an emotional third dimension by the overtones from these allusions. The several impressions or meanings given together parallel the devices of James Joyce. When the references are to even less familiar works, however, obscurity automatically ensues.

What strange education could produce an audience, no matter how limited, which, knowing French, Italian, Provençal, Latin, and Sanskrit, might enjoy the string of references at the close of *The Waste Land*:

London Bridge is falling down falling down falling down
Poi s'ascose nel foco che gli affina
Quando fiam uti chelidon—O swallow swallow
Le Prince d'Aquitaine à la tour abolie
These fragments I have shored against my ruins
Why then Ile fit you. Hieronymo's mad againe.
Datta. Dayadhvam. Damyatta.
Shantih shantih shantih

To savor these references (all noted by Eliot), it is necessary to know the *context* of the borrowed lines. When the context is known, the quotation takes on some validity. Thus the line *"Poi s'ascose,"* etc., appears in an extract from Dante quoted by Eliot in his own notes, where the three preceding lines clarify the point and indicate the state of

mind of the poet Eliot in this emotional crisis with which
The Waste Land concludes:

> 'Ara vos prec per aquella valor
> que vos guida al som de l'escalina,
> Sovegna vos a temps de ma dolor.'
> Poi s'ascose nel foco che gli affina.

Eliot translates these Provençal lines from Arnaut Daniel
in his essay on Dante: "'And so I pray you, by that Virtue
which leads you to the topmost of the stair—be mind-
ful in due time of my pain.' Then dived he back into that
fire which refines them." [67]

For the following line, however, Eliot gives merely a
reference to *Pervigilium Veneris,* although, like the Dante
allusion, the surrounding lines are necessary for adequate
understanding:

> iam loquaces ore rauco stagna cygni perstrepunt:
> adsonat Terei puella subter umbram populi,
> ut putes motus amoris ore dici musico,
> et neges queri sororem de marito barbaro.
>
> illa cantat: nos tacemus. quando ver venit meum?
> quando fiam uti chelidon ut tacere desinam?
> perdidi musam tacendo; nec me Phoebus respicit:
> sic Amyclas, quum tacerent, perdidit silentium.
>
> cras amet qui numquam amavit:
> quisque amavit, cras amet.

The lines may be rendered:

> Now the cygnets' raucous croakings break into the
>   silent marsh;

Underneath the poplar's shadow sings Tereus'
nightingale,
Telling of the flood of passion with so musical a
tongue,
You would say no sister here is wailing of her sav-
age mate.

She is singing, we are silent: when will Springtime
come to me?
When shall I be like the swallow, when shall my
voice too be heard?
I have lost the Muse by silence, and Apollo turns
from me:
Thus Amycle, sworn to silence, by its silence met
its end.

You will love, if you have not loved:
If you have loved, you will love.

It may be that the identification of lines is of some help to
a reader willing to expand the references. But this is very
considerable scaffolding for any poem. Some of the other
notes in *The Waste Land* are almost perversely pretentious;
the poetic value to be acquired from a line of poetry which
needs the following note of explication is questionable:

Drip drop drip drop drop drop drop

357. This is *Turdus aonalaschkae pallasii,* the hermit-
thrush which I have heard in Quebec County. Chapman says (*Handbook of Birds of Eastern North
America*) "it is most at home in secluded woodland
and thickety retreats. . . . Its notes are not remarkable
for variety or volume, but in purity and sweetness of

tone and exquisite modulation they are unequalled."
Its "water-dripping song" is justly celebrated.

We could add such a note to any similar line and have
criticasters rhapsodize about it, as, for example, on the
lines in "Of the Awful Battle of the Pekes and the Pollicles"
in *Old Possum's Book of Practical Cats*:

> Bark bark bark bark
> Bark bark BARK BARK

T. H. Thompson has no doubt said the last word on
such poetry in his tongue-in-cheek reconstruction of the five
scattered allusions to Sweeney into a detective story, when
he satirizes line 204 of *The Waste Land*:

> As the nightingales tell us Sweeney 'rudely forced' his
> way in and committed the act he had premeditated.
> The 'rudely forced' passage may refer to the actual
> immersion of Miss Porter, and the line which immedi-
> ately precedes it:
> > Jug jug jug jug jug jug
> would then represent onomatopoetically the sound of
> the lysol being poured into the bath from a jug.[68]

The difference between the effect of the two sets of quotations from *The Waste Land* (the "Mrs. Porter" and the
"London Bridge" passages) is one of degree, not kind. The
second produces not a new compound but a very tenuous
mixture. It is simply beyond any reader to recognize the
"feelings, phrases, images" which Eliot has chosen: "The
poet's mind is in fact a receptacle for seizing and storing up
numberless feelings, phrases, images, which remain there

until all the particles which can unite to form a new compound are present together." [69] Such lines are Eliot's communication to Eliot, and to that small group with the time and resources and desire to follow him.

Eliot seems to have deliberately sought out an elite for an audience. He has rejected the tradition that poetry should be a means of communication between the poet and a public audience, a tradition which in English began with *Beowulf*, and continued through Chaucer and Langland, Shakespeare and Milton, Dryden even, Cowper, Wordsworth and Coleridge, Scott, Byron, Shelley, Keats, Tennyson, and Browning. Eliot partly rationalizes his turning his back on common humanity, in what may be taken as a piece of personal explanation. In his *The Use of Poetry,* discussing the continually decreasing audience for poetry since Dryden's day, he says:

> But the part of society to which Dryden's work, and that of the Restoration comedians, could immediately appeal constituted something like an intellectual aristocracy; when the poet finds himself in an age in which there is no intellectual aristocracy, when power is in the hands of a class so democratic that whilst still a class it represents itself to be the whole nation; *when the only alternatives seem to be to talk to a coterie or to soliloquise,* the difficulties of the poet and the necessity of criticism become greater.[70] [My italics.]

Even his earlier poetry was addressed to coteries. His later work consists of soliloquies, as in his autobiographical lines in the third of *Four Quartets, East Coker* (1941):

> So here I am, in the middle years, having had
> twenty years—
> Twenty years largely wasted, the years of *l'entre
> deux guerres*—
> Trying to learn to use words, and every attempt
> Is a wholly new start, and a different kind of failure
> Because one has only learnt to get the better of
> words
> For the one thing no longer has to say, or the
> way in which
> One is no longer disposed to say it.

Sometimes, however, the coterie, to whom he addresses his soliloquies, after considerable intellectual jugglery not too dissimilar from the skill involved in solving a *Saturday Review of Literature* "double-crostic," may partly comprehend the more difficult personal allusions and literary references. Wolf Mankowitz, after a lengthy analysis of *Gerontion,* has to admit that "it is difficult to know how so complex a work as *Gerontion* can be approached other than through the most detailed written examination." [71] The difficulty, not only of the early but of the latest poems, is indicated by Miss Helen Gardner:

> The publication of the *Quartets* in one volume has made their interpretation easier in one way but more difficult in another. Read consecutively each illuminates the others, and the symbols employed become richer and more solid with repetition; but the cross references between the poems are now seen to be so various, subtle and complex that formal interpretation seems more than ever clumsy and impertinent, and

may even mislead readers, by appearing to impose a
logical scheme on poems which continually escape
from the logic of discourse into something nearer to
the conditions of musical thought.[72]

How much Eliot intends a reader to gain from recognition of his literary sources is an open question, especially when he does not supply the source of his allusions. It is as if, shunning real experience, Eliot had to obtain an indirect experience of life by referring to other works of art—as if these were life itself! We may apply to Eliot what he said of Swinburne: "It is, in fact, the word that gives him the thrill, not the object." [73] Eliot seems unable to face reality on its own terms, and has to use other men's mastery to help him with his own poetic experience. Yet reliance on words rather than on the experience of life avails little. In Section Five of "Burnt Norton" Eliot dwells on the hollowness of words: they

> Crack and sometimes break, under the burden,
> Under the tension, slip, slide, perish,
> Decay with imprecision. . . .

The question of plagiarism has not been raised, for has not Eliot said, "Immature poets imitate, mature poets steal"?[74] But a reader might be pardoned for not immediately recognizing when parallel lines serve as a technique of recall to achieve the Joycean literary third dimension; when they are an example of second-hand sensitivity which keeps the poet in the library safe from contact with reality; or when they are simply a "steal."

For example, Eliot frequently resorts to the (Latin) writings of St. John of the Cross. Toward the end of "Burnt Norton" are these lines by Eliot:

> In order to arrive at what you do not know
> You must go by a way which is the way of ig-
> norance.
> In order to possess what you do not possess
> You must go by the way of dispossession.
> In order to arrive at what you are not
> You must go through the way in which you are
> not.

It is interesting to compare these lines with the words and phrases of Allison Peers' translation:[75]

> In order to arrive at that which thou knowest not,
> Thou must go by a way that thou knowest not.
> In order to arrive at that which thou possessest not,
> Thou must go by a way that thou possessest not.
> In order to arrive at that which thou art not,
> Thou must go through that which thou art not.

What at first sight appears to be a genuine personalized feeling, for example, the opening of the Ariel Poem No. 8, "Journey of the Magi":

> 'A cold coming we had of it
> Just the worst time of the year
> For a journey, and such a long journey:
> The ways deep and the weather sharp,
> The very dead of winter.'

is only the editing of the seventeenth-century prose of Lancelot Andrewes: "It was no summer progress. A cold coming they had of it at this time of the year, just the worst time of the year to take a journey, and specially a long journey in. The ways deep, the weather sharp, the days short, the sun farthest off, *in solstitio brumali,* 'the very dead of winter.' " [76]

Other examples of such relationships are continually being brought to light. The first fifty lines of Part II of *The Waste Land* have been shown to be indebted to Conrad's short story, *The Return;*[77] half a dozen lines in *Gerontion* are based on lines in Cardinal Newman's *Dream of Gerontius,* and single lines in this poem are taken from *The Education of Henry Adams* and works by Lancelot Andrewes.[78] Four lines in *Murder in the Cathedral* are taken from Conan Doyle's *The Musgrave Ritual.*[79]

Eliot has drawn a false scent for the pursuers of prototypes of *The Cocktail Party* by telling them that Euripides' *Alcestis* gave him the pattern. He admits that he had to "go into detailed explanation" to convince some readers of the resemblances. There is, however, a much closer parallel, namely, Charles Williams' novel, *Descent into Hell* (1937). The basic theme is parallel—the quest of a young woman, Pauline Anstruther (of whom *The Cocktail Party's* Celia is a parallel), for personal integration. This she achieves by "communication" with the spirits of the dead, under the guidance of a successful middle-aged poetic dramatist, Peter Stanhope, who resembles Dr. Harcourt-Reilly. Indeed, one description of him might serve as a stage direction for Reilly describing the death of Celia: "His voice became incantation; his hand stretched upward in the air, as if he invoked the motion of the influences, and the hand was magical to her sight." Stanhope prefigures Reilly in another way. At the end of each consultation (generally by telephone), he advises Pauline, "Go with God" or "Go in peace." *The Cocktail Party's* meddling Julia has a counterpart in the interfering old woman, Lily Sammile, who seems to know much about other people's lives. She frequents a graveyard. Pauline, unlike Celia, is not martyred; but she identifies herself with her seventeenth-century Protestant ancestor who "had gone willingly to death, chosen it, insisted on it" in the religious persecutions of Queen Mary. As he was being burnt, "He gave a loud cry and said: *I have seen the salvation of my God,* and so many times till he died. . . ."

> Pauline shuddered. 'It was a terrible thing,' she said. 'How he could shout for joy like that!'
> 'Salvation,' Mrs. Anstruther said mildly, 'is quite often a terrible thing—a frightening good.'

Many phrases of *The Cocktail Party* are reminiscent of *Descent into Hell*: Eliot himself might have written "But if the past still lives in its own present beside our present . . ." or "The point of his return was not determined by himself, but by his salvation, by a direction not yet formulated, by the economy of means of the Omnipotence. . . ." Far from explaining anything, Williams too has his character say: "She laughed again at the useless attempt to explain." What is especially notable is the use of the same passage from Shelley's *Prometheus Unbound* (Act I, 190-199) as the key to both works. Reilly quotes the lines, beginning

> Ere Babylon was dust
> The magus Zoroaster, my dead child,
> Met his own image walking in the garden. . . .

at the climax of *The Cocktail Party,* where he relates how
Celia died. In *Descent into Hell* these lines form a frame,
and are quoted and discussed on no less than five separate
occasions.[81] Charles Williams's novels are all published by
the firm, Faber and Faber, where Eliot is an editor and di-
rector, and might therefore be familiar to him as publisher.
Williams is not so remote as Euripides.

So we find, in spite of denials, a cult of obscurity. And
coteries in the little magazines maintain that a muddy
stream of consciousness is poetry. No doubt each group derives satisfaction from having solved Eliot's riddles and interpreted them better than the next. Harold Laski, with
that eminent common sense he applied to literary criticism,
put his finger very neatly on these snobs when, apropos of
Eliot's personalized language, he wrote: "But I suspect that
the satisfaction he has given them derives less from the inherent beauty of what he has written than from the fact
that, as they apprehend the meaning of his exotic remote-
ness, they are made to feel that they, too, by that power to
apprehend, are set apart, with their master, from the multi-
tude." [82]

Finally there is one more development of Eliot's allusions
and overtones which gives trouble to his readers. Unques-
tionably symbols, hints, recollections are valuable in poetry.
A poet, however, should know when to use direct, when indirect, statement; when to use ornament, when to leave

his work unadorned; when to use wit, when to rely on simple emotion. Often Eliot is oblique on subjects where obliquity is unsuitable. The serious reader toils after the poet's intention, only to find a simple statement, better suited to prose expression.

Professor E. M. W. Tillyard has recently drawn attention to the dangers of this "disguised statement," as he calls it, where what could be better said in direct poetry (which may be embroidered or ornamented) is said in symbols or allusions: "A good deal of recent English verse has accepted Mallarmé's doctrine and the obligation to be oblique at any cost; with the result that some of it, naturally belonging to the province of statement, masquerades as obliquity; and among the more serious practitioners as well as among the Enoch Soameses." [83]

Tillyard then gives some examples of this "crime," including an analysis of some lines in *Gerontion*:

> After such knowledge, what forgiveness? Think
> now
> History has many cunning passages, contrived corridors
> And issues, deceives with whispering ambitions,
> Guides us by vanities. Think now
> She gives when our attention is distracted
> And what she gives, gives with such supple confusions
> That the giving famishes the craving. Gives too late
> What's not believed in, or if still believed
> In memory only, reconsidered passion. Gives too
> soon

> Into weak hands, what's thought can be dis-
> pensed with
> Till the refusal propagates a fear.

Here the verse, elaborately imitated from Tourneur
or some other late Elizabethan dramatist (the words
'the giving famishes the craving' have an air of pasti-
che about them, unless they are an actual quotation),
suggests some subtle state of mind. But no amount of
re-reading or goodwill has revealed anything at all
subtle. On the contrary, all this talk about history re-
minds one of the author's essay on *Tradition and the
Individual Talent,* and the post-Elizabethan form is
the inappropriate and laboriously wrought receptacle
of ideas already existing: disguised statement, a bogus
obliquity.[84]

Contempt for communication in Eliot's plays (in addition
to the obscurity and obscurantism of plot and characterization) takes the form of repeated statements on the impossi-
bility of understanding the purpose of the action or the
motives of the characters as well as statements by the main
characters that they themselves cannot explain the significance.

These statements, convenient for one who either has nothing of any value to say to the world or is a little fearful of
what he is saying, sometimes appear as glorification of ignorance. In *Murder in the Cathedral,* for example, the
chorus says, "We Are afraid in a fear which we cannot
know, which we cannot face, which none understands."
The Tempter's words repeat those of Thomas himself:

> You know and do not know, what it is to act or
> suffer.
> You know and do not know, that acting is suffer-
> ing,
> And suffering action.

Thomas emphasizes the difficulties of meaning:

> Those who do not the same
> How should they know what I do?
> How should you know what I do?

This highfalutin trick of asserting ignorance as a form of
holy innocence to suggest profound spiritual depths to the
cowed reader occurs also in both *The Family Reunion*
and *The Cocktail Party*. The "I don't know, but it's deep
stuff" motif reappears throughout *The Family Reunion*
from page 18 with Gerald's "I don't in the least know what
you're talking about," to page 131 with Violet's lines:

> You do not know what has been going on, Ivy.
> And if you did, you would not understand it.
> I do not understand it, so how could you?

There is generally no *dramatic* justification for these
comments (save perhaps to show the vapidity of the characters); their purpose seems to be conscious obfuscation to
overawe the critics. Harry tells Mary,[85] who with Agatha
and Downing is the only other character to *see* the Furies,
"You do not know, You cannot know, you cannot understand." When Mary replies that she might learn, if he
were patient with her, Harry retorts:

> If I tried to explain, you could never understand:
> Explaining would only make a worse misunder-
>   standing;
> Explaining would only set me farther away from
>   you.

What would we think of the heroes of Shakespeare, undergoing as critical mental battles as any that Harry went
through, if all they could say was "You don't understand
me. You cannot understand me" (p. 93). Would Hamlet,
whose doubts of the righteousness of his actions parallel
Harry's, have nothing more to say than:

> But I cannot explain that to you now. . . .
> But at present, I cannot explain it to anyone:
> I do not know the words in which to explain it—
> That is what makes it harder.

In Harry, who is not able to explain to sympathetic characters in the play this great mystery, which has freed him
from those feelings of guilt which were ruining his life,
Eliot has shown his incapacity to make a religious experience intelligible and valid.

Eliot's latest attempt in *The Cocktail Party* is no more
successful than those in the two earlier plays. Speaking generally in the person of Sir Henry Harcourt-Reilly, the psychiatrist or priest, Eliot dwells on this "unknowing." He
answers Lavinia's questions about Celia's death agony:

> But such experience can only be hinted at
> In myths and images. To speak about it
> We talk of darkness, labyrinths, Minotaur terrors.

Earlier, describing to Celia how she may obtain "peace of mind," Reilly tells her that there is an alternative way to that which the Chamberlaynes, for example, might follow; but she will need courage because *this* way is unknown and cannot be described "in familiar terms." So it requires

> The kind of faith that issues from despair.
> The destination cannot be described;
> You will know very little until you get there;
> You will journey blind. But the way leads towards possession
> Of what you have sought for in the wrong place.

The effect of these lines is to wrap up the "moral" in seemingly "significant" but meaningless symbols. An account of experience that can only be "hinted at In myths and images," that to the modern world is void of sense, casts doubt on the validity of both experience and writer.

In *The Cocktail Party,* as in *The Family Reunion,* there are many occasions when, in conversational exchanges, the characters talk of mystery, not knowing, and not understanding, from the first instance (on page 35 of the printed play) by Julia that

> There's altogether too much mystery
> About this place today

to the last on page 179, by Peter:

> I'm sorry. I don't believe I've taken in
> All that you've been saying. . . .

and covering a long series of "I don't know what has happened" (Edward, p. 52), "I'm completely in the dark" (Edward, p. 76), "It's all delightfully mysterious" (Celia, p. 132), and "I understand nothing" (Peter, p. 177). Although these statements occur naturally in the course of the dialogue, we must remember that Eliot chose to create the situations which produced them, and they certainly emphasize the illusion of obscurity and mystery.

To throw at an audience such terms as "scolding hills," "the quicksand," "stone passages," or "smoky wilderness" to express the difficulties of the spiritual journey is to invite uncommunication. If the audience were contemplatives, versed in such mystical writings as Eliot has consulted (such as *The Cloud of Unknowing,* which he seems to refer to at least twice in *The Family Reunion*),[86] these metaphors might explain certain mental states. But they are meaningless on any public stage. Equally meaningless are the incantations which are recited in both of the later plays:

The Family Reunion	*The Cocktail Party*
This way the pilgrimage	Protector of travellers
Of expiation	Bless the road
Round and round the circle	
Completing the charm	Watch over her in the desert
So the knot be unknotted	Watch over her in the mountain
The crossed be uncrossed	
The crooked be made straight	Watch over her in the labyrinth
And the curse be ended	Watch over her in the quicksand
By intercession	
By pilgrimage	
By those who depart	Protect her from the Voices
In several directions	Protect her from the Visions

The Family Reunion	*The Cocktail Party*
For their own redemption	Protect her in the tumult
And that of the departed—	Protect her in the silence
May they rest in peace	Go in peace, my daughter.
	Work out your salvation with diligence.

There is one final point which may summarize the Eliot view of audience communication as presented in these plays. In *The Cocktail Party,* Reilly, the Guardian, who takes it on his responsibility to direct human lives (and deaths), says

> And when I say to one like her
> 'Work out your salvation with diligence,' I do not understand
> What I myself am saying.

Harry, in *The Family Reunion,* on entering this Eliot state of blissful ignorance, says too:

> Whether I know what I am saying, or why I say it
> That does not matter.

Not only in poetry, but even when he has at his disposal 128 pages of prose, Eliot is unable to make clear in his own mind what he is out to do. Like Harry and Reilly, he says, in fact, "I don't know what I am talking about." In the *Notes towards the Definition of Culture,* speaking in the first person, Eliot writes: "The way of looking at culture and religion which I have been trying to adumbrate is so difficult that I am not sure I grasp it myself except in flashes, or that I comprehend all its implications." [87]

Yet Eliot knows the laws of the theater well enough to give good advice to other practitioners. Reviewing Ronald Duncan's play, *The Dull Ass's Hoof,* Eliot listed theoretical principles the very opposite of his own practice of obscurity:

> The conditions I mean are that there must be a plot with a perfectly clear meaning, however many other meanings may be hidden behind it, and that the language also, and every speech that is not a lyrical interlude, should have a perfectly clear and immediately apprehensible meaning, the relation of which (or the irrelevance of which) to the action should not be obscure. I also believe that if a play is to be readable, it must be *intended* for the stage.[88]

Eliot, however, when seized by the impulse to write mystical propaganda or to fit characterization to a belief in original sin, disregards what he knows. None of his plots has "a perfectly clear meaning," nor has his language anywhere "a perfectly clear and immediately apprehensible meaning," the two main conditions he postulated for theatrical success. With Eliot, dramatic technique has been subordinated to a preconceived philosophy.

It is perhaps a little more difficult to be obscure in prose where symbols and allusions are not commonly employed; but Eliot manages that, too. He shows his contempt for communication in his essays in a number of ways. For example, he reverses his opinions (sometimes in the same paragraph), and makes sweeping comments without giving any reasons or documentation for his opinions.

Eliot's reversals of opinions are well-known. Since the

thirties, he has reversed himself on many issues. He now praises Milton, Tennyson, and Yeats who, in 1933, had "a somewhat artificially induced poeticality." [89] What is disturbing is that Eliot's adulators find Eliot a great critic both when he praises and dismisses Milton, Tennyson, or Yeats.

Less well known are those frequent self-contradictions, and those literary precepts which contradict, and are contradicted by, his poetic practice. The reader is confronted with a Janus, never knowing which way Eliot is facing, and when he is talking out of the back of his head. Under the normal processes of maturity, increased reading and experience, we should expect a critic's opinions to be modified as he becomes aware of new evidence. Eliot's overall political and philosophic views have certainly changed, and if, as I am suggesting here, they have changed for the worse, then his literary abilities, which are part of the whole man, cannot have developed as we should have hoped.

One who is claimed by so many critics to be England's leading poet should be able to define poetry, and say whether or not verse is essential. In 1917, he says that poetry must be written in (metrical) verse: "after much reflection I conclude that the only absolute distinction to be drawn is that poetry is written in verse, and prose is written in prose." [90] Yet in this very same essay, he says that Dante and Rimbaud both wrote poetry, although the former used verse and the latter prose. Again in 1921, he writes, "I do not assume the identification of poetry with verse." [91] This opinion lasted until 1930, when, in the preface to St. John Perse's *Anabase,* he says poetry could be written either in verse or prose.[92] But by 1933, Eliot had spun the circle back to his 1917 position: "What is 'all poetry'? Everything written in verse which a sufficient number of the best minds have considered to be poetry." [93]

These anomalies occur for the most part in different essays, even though they may be almost contemporaneous. When opposite views occur in one and the same essay, as Yvor Winters has also shown,[94] we need look for no further explanation than a confused intellect.

One gross illustration of unreason[95] occurs in his essay on "Blake" in *The Sacred Wood*. On one page he says (speaking of Blake) that the education of an artist is hindered and harmed, when it is the ordinary sort of acquisition of impersonal ideas designed to force him to conform to society. Three pages later, Eliot says (speaking of Blake) that what an artist needs is the control of a respect for impersonal reason, for common sense, and the control of a framework of accepted and traditional ideas. Here are the two passages, printed in parallel columns, the first proclaiming that impersonal values and conformity are bad; the second that impersonal values and conformity are good.

It is important that the artist should be highly educated in his own art; but his education is one that is hindered rather than helped by the ordinary processes of society which constitute education for the ordinary man. For these processes consist largely in the acquisition of im-

Blake was endowed with a capacity for considerable understanding of human nature, with a remarkable and original sense of language and the music of language, and a gift of hallucinated vision. Had these been controlled by a respect for impersonal reason, for

personal ideas which obscure what we really are and feel, what we really want, and what really excites our interest. It is of course not the actual information acquired, but the conformity which the accumulation of knowledge is apt to impose, that is harmful.[96]

common sense, for the objectivity of science, it would have been better for him. What his genius required, and what it sadly lacked, was a framework of accepted and traditional ideas which would have prevented him from indulging in a philosophy of his own, and concentrated his attention upon the problems of the poet.[97]

And Eliot has achieved the literary distinction of contradicting himself in the same sentence, as was first pointed out by Ernest Sutherland Bates.[98] In "Imperfect Critics," also in *The Sacred Wood,* Eliot wrote: "And whatever our opinion of Swinburne's verse, the notes upon poets by a poet of Swinburne's dimensions must be read with attention and respect."[99] If this sentence means anything, it says that although Swinburne is an inferior poet, we must pay attention to his criticism because Swinburne is a superior poet. It is unlikely that Eliot would use "dimensions" for Swinburne's physical size; the word may mean "vast bulk of compositions." If this is the meaning, it implies that quantity becomes quality. If it means "magnitude" or "importance," as the word is generally taken, then the sentence is even more obviously nonsense.

It is difficult to reconcile Eliot's poetic practice with his poetic theory. Eliot says, in his critical works, that great poets should be generally understood: "It is true, I believe, that in a healthy society, the really great poet should be understood in part, and responded to, by compatriots of the humblest, as well as by those of the highest level of culture."[100] Perhaps our society is not healthy enough, but is Eliot's poetry understood, even in part, by men of the humblest, or for that matter the higher levels of culture?

Eliot in one place says great poets should be representative of their age. The great poet must "express with individual differences the general state of mind, not as *duty*, but simply because he cannot help participating in it."[101] Again, Eliot writes: "The great poet, in writing himself, writes his time. Thus Dante, hardly knowing it, became the voice of the thirteenth century; Shakespeare, hardly knowing it, became the representative of the end of the sixteenth century, of a turning point in history."[102]

Yet Eliot has gone to great lengths to show that his own age does not agree with him, and that his philosophy is not representative of the twentieth century:

> The problem of leading a Christian life in a non-Christian society is now very present to us. . . . It is not merely the problem of a minority in a society of *individuals* holding an alien belief. . . . And as for the Christian who is not conscious of his dilemma—and he is in the majority—he is becoming more and more de-Christianized by all sorts of unconscious pressure: paganism holds all the most valuable advertising space.[103]

If Eliot is so out of step with current trends of thought as he says, he is (by his own definition) not a great poet! It

may have been a belated awareness of the difficulty of reconciling precept and practice that led Eliot in 1941 to the
about-face in: "a poet who appears to be wholly out of
touch with his age may still have something very important to say to it." [104]

Another volte-face appears in the two versions of "The
Social Function of Poetry." In the 1945 version, Eliot said
that great poets should give pleasure to very many people.[105] This directly contradicted the earlier (1943) version:
"It matters little whether a poet had a large audience in his
own time. What matters is that there should always be at
least a small audience for him in every generation." [106]
Apart from deciding which of these standards to apply to
Eliot, the ordinary reader might be led to question Eliot's
reliability as a literary critic.

The contempt for people and for any direct communication with them that is to be seen in other aspects of Eliot's
work is also at the bottom of his doctrinaire statements, delivered *ex cathedra,* without any pretense of justifying docu-
menting, or explaining them. This habit in his earlier essays
gave offense to many readers, which Eliot acknowledged in
the Preface to the 1928 edition of *The Sacred Wood* (first
published in 1920): "There are, it is true, faults of style
which I regret; and especially I detect frequently a stiff-
ness and an assumption of pontifical solemnity which may
be tiresome to many readers." [107] But the dogmatism continued. In *The Idea of a Christian Society* we read: "It is
only in a society with a religious basis—which is not the
same thing as an ecclesiastical despotism—that you can get

the proper harmony and tension, for the individual or for the community." [108]

No evidence is given for this absolute statement; and in the absence of any evidence, it must be taken as a piece of arrogance. This book, like the *Notes towards the Definition of Culture,* is full of such arrogant dicta.

Inconsequential opinions are frequently presented in almost laughably ceremonious tones. This pontification, particularly on cultural topics, shows a supercilious arrogation of authority, as in this pronouncement: "We discern three tendencies in education as in politics, the *liberal,* the *radical,* and what I am tempted to call, perhaps simply because it is my own, the *orthodox.*" [109] In the *Notes,* Eliot similarly rules out interpretations other than his own, appropriating a common term to his private uses:

> What I try to say is this: here are what I believe to be essential conditions for the growth and for the survival of culture. If they conflict with any passionate faith of the reader—if, for instance, he finds it shocking that culture and equalitarianism should conflict, if it seems monstrous to him that anyone should have 'advantages of birth'—I do not ask him to change his faith, I merely ask him to stop paying lip-service to culture.[110]

Who is this Eliot to forbid the use of the word *culture* except in his own purely personalized definition? In such an attitude we see not a scholar balancing various points of view, but the overbearing trial examiner, perhaps not too secure of his stand.

This doctrinaire arrogance also appears in the plays. On Dr. Reilly the manner fits like a glove. How pompous he is, recommending what is commonly called in England "mother's ruin," telling Edward that he likes his gin mixed with

> Nothing but water.
> And I recommend you the same prescription. . . .
> Let me prepare it for you, if I may. . . .
> Strong . . . but sip it slowly . . . and drink it sitting down.
> Breathe deeply, and adopt a relaxed position.
> There we are.

Once the worm turns, and Edward, a lawyer, gets nettled:

> And please don't suggest.
> I have often used these terms in examining witnesses,
> So I don't like them. May I put it to *you*? . . .
> I think your speculations rather offensive.

From pontification and arrogance, this contempt for men leads also to outright deception of the reader. I have already given some examples of this technique, where Eliot assumes a guise of scrupulous fairness in presenting both sides of a problem. "Execrating" fascism, for example, Eliot holds up its efficiency for admiration.[111] In another passage in *The Idea of a Christian Society,* discussing the foundations of morality necessary in a society, Eliot again compares fascism with Western democracy: "we may reflect, that a good deal of the attention of totalitarian states has been devoted, with a steadiness of purpose not always found in democracies, to providing their national life with a foundation of morality—the wrong kind perhaps, but a good deal more of it."[112]

This pretense of impartiality enables Eliot to deflect criticism, without changing his original position. In the introduction to the collection of essays entitled *For Lancelot Andrewes* (1928), Eliot has stated his belief in the well-known catchphrase, "The general point of view may be described as classicist in literature, royalist in politics, and anglo-catholic in religion." [113] From the 1936 edition Eliot omitted three of the original essays, and added another five, calling the new volume *Essays Ancient and Modern*. The preface was also omitted. In *After Strange Gods* (1934), Eliot discusses the public reaction to this preface.

> I may as well admit at this point that in this discussion of terms I have my own log to roll. Some years ago, in the preface to a small volume of essays, I made a sort of summary declaration of faith in matters religious, political and literary. The facility with which this statement has been quoted has helped to reveal to me as it stands the statement is injudicious. It may suggest that the three subjects are of equal importance to me, which is not so; it may suggest that I accept all three beliefs on the same grounds, which is not so; and it may suggest that I believe that they all hang together or fall together, which would be the most serious misunderstanding of all. That there are connexions for me I of course admit, but these illuminate my own mind rather than the external world; and I now see the danger of suggesting to outsiders that the

> Faith is a political principle or a literary fashion, and
> the sum of all a dramatic posture.[114]

We see how beguiling arguments and qualifications evade
the issue: the original sentence is a forthright slogan for reaction. "The 'open' mind is most easily enslaved." Eliot has
given the appearance of reconsidering his stand, but actually
he has not changed at all. Eliot merely says, not that he is
dissatisfied with the preface, nor that he repudiates it, but
that he takes the opportunity "of omitting the preface,
which had more than served its turn."[115] This could
mean anything. In the "retraction" Eliot tries to disarm the
critic by admitting he has his "own log to roll." The quot-
ability has "helped" to reveal to him—did anything else
help? The statement "as it stands"—is Eliot going to change
it, amend it, or deny it altogether?—is "injudicious"—what
does this mean: lacking qualities of judicious thought? or
merely (as the note in *Essays Ancient and Modern* would
imply) ill-timed, or ill-advised? Then Eliot parries criticism
that it was a *reactionary* credo, by saying that it suggests
three possibilities. Actually it suggests them only because
Eliot has chosen these three out of other possibilities. Finally, Eliot in effect says that this statement is a personal
matter, or, at most, only a matter to those not outside his
Faith. But what a public figure says is of concern to others
than his own friends.

Another pseudo-objective effect, which leaves even a careful reader befuddled, is Eliot's introduction of qualifier
after qualifier into his sentences, a sort of veneer of disin-
terestedness. A related technique to justify ignoring the necessity for choice is the over-protestation of the fair mind—

especially when the choice must logically go to principles discomfiting to Eliot's beliefs. In a recent article we have a remarkable example of sentences so hedged with every conceivable delimitation as to leave the reader almost at a complete loss to know just what Eliot means. It shows how ready Eliot is to escape into unreason in order to avoid making a choice. In an interview reported in the British magazine *Horizon,* now defunct, on the subject, "The Condition of Man Today," Eliot was asked, "Do you, on the whole, believe in the creative future of the white race?" The basis of the question was the suggestion that "changes brought about by science and technology have brought a change in the thinking power of mankind." Here is Eliot's answer quoted in full:

> I think it is possible that that process of which you speak and of which many thoughtful people have been aware may certainly go still further than we know at present in the same direction, but I think that any tendency like that gives rise to its own opposite and that in the end, sooner or later, and in one way or another there will be a general rebellion against that, because, you see, that sort of thing leads to something which the technological type of mind leaves out of account. And that is, that human beings will just become bored with the kind of life they have from it—and I think that boredom is a very powerful force in life and that people will do the most extraordinary things to escape from it. They may not act rationally, of course, in getting out of it, and that will raise psychological difficulties which will express themselves in due course.[116]

The formulation of the question (judged by the explanation given at the head of the interview) is itself unclear and actually completely nondiscussable: "changes" (a very neutral word with no connotation of "advances") in science and technology have resulted in changes in man's "thinking power" (this is vague: does the change result in increased or decreased thinking power? what does thinking power mean—ability to invent and control more technological developments? or ability to think philosophically, abstractly? or to produce art? or what?). Eliot's answer, however, multiplies the confusion. The "process" *may* go *still* further in the same direction—there may be a continuation? or an increase of scientific changes with corresponding changes in man's thinking power? or there will be more changes in man's thinking power? *But* "any tendency like that" (the original process or the tendency toward "going still further"?) "gives rise to its own opposite." Does this clause mean the opposite of increase, that is, decrease? or that scientific change will *not* change man's thinking power? *What* is "that sort of thing" that leads to "something"?

It should be clear by now that Eliot's fastidious disdain for those who have not had his advantages manifests itself in his writings as obscurity. In charging "obscurity" I am not suggesting that a poet must write to be understood by each and all; in our civilization poetry is no longer a popular mass medium. But one is entitled to ask that the poet shall be intelligible to those who have a desire to read him and are prepared to devote some effort to appreciation, cognizant that as much time and care may go into the making of a few hundred lines of poetry as into a long novel.

But few people are willing to make this effort, in an age which even in its literature demands quick results. Poets, sensing this public neglect and, *qua* authors, having something of value to say to the world, are moving out of the seemingly limited modes of poetry into what is the prevailing literary form of our century, the novel. In the twentieth century, for the first time we have some authors who have written sufficient poetry to demonstrate that they might have become as celebrated poets as they were prose writers— Meredith, Hardy, Henry James, Mary Webb, and, with lesser poetic productivity, D. H. Lawrence, James Joyce, Ruthven Todd, Osbert Sitwell. The shift of Aragon, one of France's two outstanding living poets, to the writing of novels is significant.

In an effort to find a larger audience, Eliot too has moved, but from poetry to poetic drama. Eliot, however, has gone from one restricted form to another (*Murder in the Cathedral* was conceived for production in a church, and not for the mass medium of the cinema). In Eliot's case, as I have tried to show, he has only transferred difficulty and obscurity from the printed page to the living stage. This fact seems to imply that his obscurity and obscurantism arise from a trend in his thinking which is bound to manifest itself in whatever he writes.

THE

ELIOT

PROBLEM

IN THE PRECEDING CHAPTERS I HAVE SOUGHT TO DISENTANGLE the actual Eliot, a poet of minor achievement, emotionally sterile and with a mind coarsened by snobbery and constricted by bigotry, from the myth which has exalted him into a great poet and an advanced cultural leader. In this chapter I explore some of the factors that went into the making of the myth and go into its continuing nurture.

The problem can best be understood in terms of the historical setting in which Eliot's work has functioned. As an immediate result of the world wars, whatever the deeper causes may be, society has been severely dislocated. Over large parts of the world social change, in some cases violent in form, has been taking place. As in other periods of social change, the Protestant Reformation, the French Revolution, etc., the pressure for change has been met by a conservative counter-pressure.

This has led to general conflict and confusion. Many have found themselves involved in conflicts, in one way or another, and called to take sides before they have had time to mature their opinions. Consequently, loyalties have been fluid and belief uncertain and there has been much renegacy with the shifts of opinions and fortunes. Eliot himself, now a pillar of established religion and order, can serve as an example. His views have changed from a repudiation of society and gibes at the church to defense of certain traditions and even of institutions long abandoned.

In such an intellectual atmosphere, objective judgment has proved difficult and has become rare. On both sides, progressive and conservative (or, in immediately contemporary terms, the Left and the Right), reputations have been inflated for polemical purposes. A characteristic example is André Gide, first inflated by the Left, then still more egregiously inflated by the Right after his renegacy from the Left.

In the West, particularly in America, control of the press, the chairs at the universities, the memberships on prize committees, etc., of all that determines the shaping of opinion and the making of reputations, has come into the hands of conservatives. The inflation of Eliot is both the chief product and the most typical example of their labors.

There is some similarity here—though there is nothing analogous in their personalities or in the nature of their work—in the inflation of Samuel Johnson, in his day, as an intellectual support of conservatism. The similarity is even more striking—though again there is nothing analogous in their personalities or their work—in the case of Edmund Waller. Now virtually unread and unknown, except to literary historians, this Royalist poet was enormously inflated during the Stuart restoration following the English revolution.

Such myth-making is, of course, not gratuitous. The Right has not been assiduous in its honors and homage to Eliot merely out of sentiments of affinity and gratitude. To so inflate him gives the impression that the titans are ranged on the Right. And through the prestige of a literary man so inflated, opinions can get a hearing that would be suspect in other spokesmen. It would be well to bear this in mind in considering the "Eliot problem."

How can the impact of Eliot on Anglo-American culture be explained? Why does this secular society, where "the modern environment is so unfavourable to faith," [1] give such praise to a man who for the past thirty years has been writing almost exclusively from a clericalist viewpoint? Why has an author with reactionary, even proto-fascist, ideas been accepted so enthusiastically in Britain and America, where most men continue to profess democratic and liberal sentiments? Why is a writer whose ecclesiastical and sociological opinions have so adversely interfered with his reflection of the world and its expression in literature still lauded so uncritically? This is the Eliot problem.

As noted above, the answers must be given in relation to the general situation. And the answers must also encompass the people among whom Eliot writes and the media of communication which link the author to his public.

One reason it has been easy to inflate Eliot's reputation is that many people who regard themselves as informed and literate, but are brought up largely on gossip columns and digests, have read little, if any, of his works. They are content to accept the evaluations of "experts." With the praises so extravagant, it is no wonder that the evaluation is accepted.

Nor is it surprising that Eliot had comparatively few readers, for he has always written in nonpopular forms and seldom intelligibly. Poems (especially as difficult as those of Eliot), verse-dramas, literary and critical essays, religious tracts, rarely become best-sellers without extrinsic aiding circumstances.

It was also easy to establish his reputation because he wrote in restricted media, where he encountered relatively few rivals. Thus Eliot was assured of some attention, irrespective of the value of what he produced. He was able to gain immediate note as a literary critic, for example, because there were few critics in the earlier twentieth century in England. Such figures as Gosse, Stephen, and Saintsbury were essentially of the nineteenth century. Some scholars achieved a measure of public recognition—W. P. Ker, O. Elton, R. W. Chambers—but the number of nonacademic critics was few. The Sitwells wrote a little criticism; Sisley Huddleston and Frank Harris were writing in Paris. Herbert Read, Clive Bell, and Wyndham Lewis sometimes turned aside from their concern with the graphic arts to literary matters. Virginia Woolf, Quiller-Couch, and Robert Graves sought to raise the reading standards of the British public. Later, Richards and Leavis and Empson gathered their disciples round them in the fens. But, when Eliot was emerging, he faced little competition. Anyone who could turn out *bons mots,* such as those of Eliot which I have previously quoted (p. 7), and could support them with textual criticism, was almost sure of a hearing.

This lack of rigorous competition holds true for his poetry as well. There, too, he had few rivals. And as for poetic drama, it is difficult to count more than a handful of writers—the Auden-Isherwood team, Gordon Bottomley, Wallace B. Nichols, Lawrence Binyon, and later Stephen Spender and Louis MacNeice. Thus in this medium, too, a solitary figure could get serious consideration, quite apart from the merit of his writing.

Furthermore, until recently, the standard anthologies of poetry included only the early and shorter Eliot poems; and it is on these and *The Waste Land* that Eliot's prestige has been built. Thus such a widely read, standard anthology as Louis Untermeyer's *Book of Living Verse* (1932, 1939, 1945) includes only poems two or three decades old: "Preludes" (1915), *"La Figlia Che Piange"* (1916), "Sweeney among the Nightingales" (1918), "The Hollow Men" (1925), and "A Song for Simeon" (1928).

Michael Roberts' *Faber Book of Modern Verse* (1936 and numerous later editions), published by Eliot's own firm, includes some of the later poems to 1932, such as "Marina," "Triumphal March," and "Difficulties of a Statesman," as well as part of *Ash Wednesday.* The most recent anthology, the *Contemporary Poets* edited by Kenneth Allot, which, because it is distributed by Penguin Books, will become a best seller, includes a preponderance of later verse: "Sweeney Erect" (1919), *The Waste Land,* Part II (1922), *Ash Wednesday,* Part VI (1930), and extracts from *Murder in the Cathedral* (1935) and *The Cocktail Party* (1949)—these two latter substituted, for reasons of copyright, for *Little Gidding*. But Allot's anthology only appeared in 1950.

Few of these readers have added much to their recollection of the early pieces which made Eliot's first reputation. They may have read *Murder in the Cathedral* (or, in America, seen it in the W.P.A. Theatre production) or seen *The Cocktail Party*. Their opinion of *Murder in the Cathedral* will not be directly influenced by the message, which they will conveniently place beyond contemporary history and forget. They will rather concentrate on the verse choruses, which are extremely clever mood studies, evoking the sense of taste and touch as effectively as that of sight. When a religious topic of the twelfth century is so skillfully dressed up, it is as easy to suspend disbelief as if a play on Confucianism were under discussion. *The Cocktail Party* is, as everybody agrees, obscure or at least difficult, but at least it is easy to laugh at its smart-set sophistication. After all, Eliot does call it a comedy. For these reasons the serious reader may tend to pass lightly over the plays.

The work of Eliot after about 1922 is thus sloughed off, and Eliot stands or falls by his earliest poems! An interesting variant of this attitude is seen among those who never liked the early Eliot. Many elderly and orthodox scholars still dismiss Eliot as an exponent of modernism, unaware that their own position and that of the present-day Eliot are no longer far apart.

Of all his early poems, the one which had the greatest impact was *The Waste Land*. It was by this poem, more than any other, that Eliot became famous. Why did it make such an appeal to the young intellectuals of the twenties, and why has its influence persisted until today, so that to many Eliot is still the poet only of *The Waste Land*?

The Waste Land, when it appeared, was taken as a symbol of the disillusion of the postwar period, and what Gertrude Stein called the "lost generation." The young university men who were the poem's loudest supporters were finding their world incapable of making use of their education or offering any challenge to their talents. For all their education, they did not realize that a once expanding economy had become, after the drain of World War I, frozen, static, moribund, a waste land producing men of straw. They did not realize that the frontiers once open to allow passage from cottage to mansion were now closed. Their training had made them "professionals," identified in interests with the ruling class. Consequently, in these early twenties, few thought of turning to social reconstruction as an alternative to decay. The vast majority simply stagnated. The cynicism and hopelessness of *The Waste Land* and "Gerontion" expressed the feelings of a large number of middle-class Englishmen and Americans. These poems were, therefore, for this one section of British and American society, "real."

So in the universities, this limited aspect of the world shown in the poem was considered an accurate picture, and most critical circles did not remark its basic limitations. The only criticism came from some intellectuals left of center (who were at least aware of standards other than those of Eliot), as, for example, Prince Mirsky's analysis of *The Waste Land* in *Echanges* in 1931.[2] Other intellectuals on the Left, however, accepted it as advanced in two senses—as a repudiation of a decayed society, and as a forward step in poetic technique.

It was indeed unfortunate for the later history of English literature that the critics of Eliot (if not Eliot himself) took this picture of a limited section of British society as typical of the whole world. The mistake was repeated with Eliot's latest play, *The Cocktail Party,* where the upper-class set with its worries is given a universal importance, its characters, as in a medieval morality play, each serving as a symbol of Everyman. If the atmosphere of despair, despondency, "wan-hope," or "accidia" had not been assumed by the intellectuals to be typical of the whole world (and that it was so regarded cannot excuse Eliot's much later denials of such intentions), and if it had been taken as a dramatic monologue or as a form of lyric poetry, *The Waste Land* would have remained an effective lyric exposition of one person's feelings. But it was considered—because it was so presented—as an objective view of the world after the war.

Not only did *The Waste Land* make an appeal to the struggling intellectuals because Eliot spoke their language; but in an effort to describe this world of breakdown, decay, and disintegration, it introduced new techniques into the writing of verse which appealed to their scholarly and aesthetic interests. With Eliot, it was not so much a question of poetic diction which attracted his concern (and the attention of poetry readers). For a century or two now we have been uncomfortable in the presence of a language reserved for poetry. Wordsworth and Coleridge's manifesto prefacing the *Lyrical Ballads* in 1801 was only one of several attempts to bring the language of poetry closer to everyday speech. Eliot followed the same road: "The poetry of a people takes its life from the people's speech and in turn gives life to it." [3] Ten years later, he was repeating this view: "Poetry must not stray too far from the ordinary everyday language which we use and hear . . . it cannot afford to lose its contact with the changing language of common intercourse." [4] How completely this intention was fulfilled is, of course, another matter. This last remark was made as late as 1942, after Eliot had for a long time been filling his poetry with the specialized jargon of ecclesiolatry.

More significant in *The Waste Land* was Eliot's handling of meter. In the earlier and later works alike, he has demonstrated that, as technician, he is capable of meeting any critics of the freeness of his verse. Indeed, he has shown he can handle traditional metrical variations, as in *Old Possum's Book of Practical Cats,* and artificial stanzaic forms like the sestina, in *Four Quartets,* with considerable virtuosity. Such skills, however, have a merely incidental significance. They do not advance the technique of poetry; they merely demonstrate Eliot's dexterity.

Where Eliot has advanced technique is in devising a unit which, while it remains verse, has the mobility of prose. Poetry with Eliot becomes a flexible medium for current expression. This type of verse is at times difficult to distinguish from prose, especially when it is heard rather than seen. It confused the reviewers of *The Cocktail Party.* Howard Barnes noted its "variety of metrical forms . . . frequently have the sound of prosaic chitchat." [5] Brooks Atkinson commented at length: "At the opening performance

I was not aware that the play was written in verse until the climactic passages which begin early in the second act and reach their peak in the last scene. Most of the dialogue sounds like prose—uncommonly precise prose, but prose nevertheless." [6] These reactions seem to be those desired by Eliot, according to his summing up of "The Aims of Poetic Drama" in his Presidential Address to the Poet's Theatre Guild in London in 1949. Giving his prescription for a successful poetic drama, he shows why it could not be written completely in prose:

> A great part, sometimes the greater part, of the kind of verse play I am imagining, could, if isolated from the rest, be said quite as well in prose. These are the parts of less intensity, those concerned with everyday affairs. I should even say that the verse, in these parts of such a play, should be unnoticeable—the audience should not be conscious of the difference from prose. But here, the purpose of the verse should be to operate upon the auditor unconsciously, so that he shall think and feel in the rhythms imposed by the poet, without being aware of what these rhythms are doing. All the time, these rhythms should be *preparing* the ear of the audience for the moments of intensity, when the emotion of the character in the play may be supposed to lift him from his ordinary discourse, until the audience feels, not that the actors are speaking verse, but that the characters in the play have been lifted up into poetry. For the effect of first-rate verse drama should be, to make us believe that there are moments in life when poetry is the *natural* form of expression of ordinary men and women. [7]

Eliot did for verse, on a small scale, much of what Joyce did for prose. The achievements and failures are parallel. Eliot's early poems were the counterpart of the new stream-of-consciousness novels. In emulating the "polysemantic verbalism" of Joyce, where the distortion of an original word provoked three or four meanings almost simultaneously, Eliot resorted to quotations, allusions, symbols, and reminiscences from previous writers. In this way, to a reader familiar with the French symbolists, the Elizabethan dramatists, Dante, and the Roman Catholic liturgy, a line would have overtones from the context of the earlier writers. This technique was new in English literature. The quotations so dear to the Elizabethan and Jacobean writers are in no sense a parallel, being merely illustrative and never an integral part of the whole.

The direction of Joyce, however, lay toward a private language, comprehensible only to the author. No reader could have had the precise experiences and knowledge which produced Joyce's books. With the amount of interpretation given to Joyce, *Ulysses* is now more or less understandable; but *Finnegan's Wake* remains a subject for academic speculation. No reader is ever certain of determining what Joyce meant, and each has to re-create the work afresh for himself. But the ability of Joyce to show the workings and free-wheelings of a mind, the loosest kind of stream-of-conscious reverie within a most formal, carefully planned frame, has no doubt affected every novelist writing after 1920.

So in the same way, Eliot's *The Waste Land* gave a hint to and encouraged Auden and Spender and their set, who in

turn have had their effect on Thomas and Madge. Dylan
Thomas is an interesting illustration of how a later writer
can profit from an earlier poet's technique and put it to entirely different purposes. In points of view, Thomas is far
removed from Eliot, and throughout his poems he stays
close to the people of the Southern Welsh mining vil-
lages. Consequently his poetry is not cultish.

After 1922, Eliot turned more and more to religious
dogma, leaving behind his first admirers. A new group,
caught up for varied reasons in opposition to socialism,
found his feudal attitudes useful. Some prefer the new Eliot
because, being reactionaries themselves, they agree with
Eliot, although they are careful to disguise their political
reasons for championing him under pretenses of objective
literary interests. A number of Eliot's present supporters
had no use for him in the early twenties, when his own
political positions were undefined. Today it is clear enough
what Eliot stands for. To these must be added admirers of
his early writing who seem to have read little of his later
works but still hold him in esteem for *The Waste Land*.
Thus his prestige is fostered in two camps, to each of which
part of his work is unwelcome.

The early Eliot is quite different from the later Eliot, although there is nothing in the beginning that denies the
later development. The separation can well be illustrated by
comparing two poems. One of the most successful attacks
on organized religion written in English is "The Hippopotamus", where the satire, although very light, hits at the
weakest aspects of the Church:[8]

The hippo's feeble steps may err
In compassing material ends,
While the True Church need never stir
To gather in its dividends.

He shall be washed as white as snow
By all the martyred virgins kist,
While the True Church remains below
Wrapt in the old miasmal mist.

Seventeen years later, in 1934, Eliot was writing, not a gay squib, but ponderous and didactic choruses in his pageant *The Rock* (which takes up one sixth of the *Collected Poems*):

For good and ill deeds belong to a man alone,
     when he stands alone on the other side of death,
But here upon earth you have the reward of the
     good and ill that was done by those who have
     gone before you.
And all that is ill you may repair if you walk to-
     gether in humble repentance, expiating the sins
     of your fathers;
And all that was good you must fight to keep with
     hearts as devoted as those of your fathers who
     fought to gain it.
The Church must be forever building, for it is for-
     ever decaying within and attacked from with-
     out;
For this is the law of life; and you must remember
     that while there is time of prosperity
The people will neglect the Temple, and in time of
     adversity they will decry it.

Why Eliot has stood by the early gibing is strange, unless he regards it as a station in his religious development. At any rate, it indicates his forte—malicious satire, in which, had he continued, he might have become a minor Pope or Dryden. The early Eliot was able.

In *The Waste Land,* Eliot, in drawing a picture of a decaying society, summed up middle-class thought. He described the world he was inhabiting as a schoolteacher, bank clerk, and editorial assistant, without fully appreciating its corruption; but he created poetry. Then he turned away from what he saw. For the past quarter of a century, while fully aware of the corruption, he has almost completely ceased to describe any objective world. Now he creates propaganda.

In his first condemnation of Western capitalism, in his prose as well as in his poetry, Eliot presents some socialist conclusions (except for his denigrating views of the workers). But Eliot never took a stand on the side of the reformers or rebels. He was not prepared to accept possible dislocation to improve society. He went elsewhere, on a road that took him to anti-rationalism, a revealed mysticism, wherein he does not have to resort to reason and where the evils in modern living (of which he is conscious) are held to be the product not of an evil society to be reformed, but of evil individuals to be led to atonement.

Eliot now expands on the private world of his own mind. He escapes from the men of the society he despaired of in the 1920's into a mystical future world of his own imaginings. He may have been moved in this direction by private personal trouble. Or a middle-class upbringing might have combined with the influence of his reading to prevent him from moving left. His indebtedness to the philosophy of T. E. Hulme is considerable. Like his disciple, Hulme discounts the value of all human activity since the Renaissance. All its thought "exhibits the same complete inability to realise the meaning of the dogma of Original Sin." [9] In his *Speculations,* Hulme attacks humanism: "In the light of these absolute values [religion], man himself is judged to be essentially limited and imperfect. He is endowed with Original Sin. . . . A man is essentially bad, he can only accomplish anything of value by discipline—ethical and political. . . . When a sense of the reality of these absolute values is lacking, you get a refusal to believe any longer in the radical imperfection of either Man or Nature. This develops logically into the belief that life is the source and measure of all values, and that man is fundamentally good. . . . This leads to a complete change in all values. The problem of evil disappears, the conception of sin loses all meaning." [10] Says Eliot simply: "I agree with what Hulme says." [11]

After 1925, Eliot's preoccupation with his formula for saving society through a return to some hierarchical, mystical religion destroys the accuracy of his vision even of middle-class society. *Ash Wednesday* has some poetic validity as the account of a man trying to find an acceptable philosophy; we can enter into the difficulties of a man looking for a foothold. But in *The Rock* and *Four Quartets* this personal element is lessened. What we have is a versified tractate. That Eliot himself may not be happy with the medium of poetry for the expression of religious and political views is indicated by the paucity of his verse and the ever-increasing volume and dominance of his philosophical essays. These later essays, which loom very large in Eliot's total production, are an intellectual blueprint for clerico-fascism.

There are other early indications of the direction Eliot was taking, among them his lack of interest in any *living* group or *living* organization. Eliot more than once derogated the bishops' resolutions at the Lambeth Conferences and labeled their thinking lazy and confused. Another was his supercilious attitude toward laboring people. His dialogue of the wives in the public house in *The Waste Land* foreshadows the unreality of the husbands in *The Rock* and the stage caricature of the chauffeur in *The Family Reunion*. Still more significant are other social prejudices which are typical of a primitive stage of fascism, his anti-Semitism, for example. At one time Eliot also showed hostility to bankers, but he never mocked them, and his criticism of the profit system was short-lived. Sometimes his support of fascist trends was forthright, as just before the 1925 British election when he wrote in a dialogue: "The best we can hope for, the only thing that can save us, is a dictator." [12] Since the beginning of the last war, Eliot has repudiated his earlier comments on the immorality of a profit system by a discreet silence. He now pleads that the present system, while not perfect, needs no major change.

His present political and philosophical position makes Eliot acceptable to any established interests. The doyens of literature and the academic Colonel Blimps have enthusiastically taken him up, eager to turn his prestige as a major man of letters into a bulwark of orthodoxy. What a contrast to the twenties, when Eliot was ignored by the pundits; when the conservative *Dublin Review* could say, as late as 1933: "If *The Waste Land* means anything to me in relation to 2030 it is that *The Waste Land* will be truly a waste land, unknown and unhonoured, leering out of the darkness at all other English poetry, which will be equally unknown and unhonoured." [13]

Today among the young intellectuals and young writers, however, Eliot is no longer the force he was. It is not merely his age that causes a diminution in influence; for other writers have had disciples at even more advanced years. Eliot is rejected by many eager and searching minds who find unsubstantiated dogma repellent. In the colleges he is today handed down by the dons; once—how long ago—he was held up by the students.

The most articulate supporters of Eliot, those who have largely created the Eliot myth in America, are the admittedly conservative group known as the Southern Agrarians. Of this group associated with the manifesto *I'll Take my Stand,* one Southern writer has commented that it appears to be known by the long list of what it opposed. "Now this, no doubt, is a fine list of things to be against except that it appeared to leave the agrarians only one thing to be for— notably the ante-bellum southern planter." [14] These writers naturally find kinship with Eliot's politics and want to spread his views. In the *Southern Review* in 1935 Tate said of Eliot's editorship: "The *Criterion* under T. S. Eliot has become the best quarterly of our time." [15] And other New Critics concur. Blackmur, for example, reviewing *Notes towards the Definition of Culture,* declares: "To most of them [Eliot's ideas] I assent. . . ." [16] I. A. Richards, now domiciled in America, says: "With most of his argument I seem to myself to be in reluctant agreement." [17]

A writer with the skill Eliot displayed in his early writings, who had a following and appealed to young men and women of the twenties, is valuable as a symbol. The "New Critics" find it useful to build up the prestige of Eliot to reinforce the prestige of their group and of other writers whose political views align them with the Eliot party. And Eliot reciprocates with praise for Tate and *I'll Take my Stand*. He does so with the omniscient air carefully built up by Tate himself. "But it is a sound and right reaction which impelled Mr. Allen Tate and his eleven Southerners to write their book." [18]

Among the Southern Agrarians the best known critics are perhaps Robert Penn Warren, Allen Tate, Cleanth Brooks, and John C. Ransom. If we look at their writings, we get some idea of what attracts them to Eliot. Here are some Tateisms which might very well have come out of Eliot:

> Religion's respect for the power of nature lies in her contempt for knowledge of it; to quantify nature is ultimately to quantify ourselves. Religion is satisfied with the dogma that nature is evil, and that our recovery from it is mysterious ("grace"). [19]

> I may look at English history with Hilaire Belloc—as I happen to do with reservations—as the decline of moral standards and human liberty from the twelfth century to our day. [20]

The traditional society is based upon property, and property means not only ownership but control. . . . A society based upon property will pass on its heritage in a concrete form, and this concrete form, property, which means moral control of the means of life, is the medium in which the tradition is passed on.[21]

The political position of the Southern Agrarians, no less than that of Eliot, would have less respect among the mass of democratic Americans were it better known. Furthermore, this position is completely at variance with the whole trend of American and British literature which, save for a few examples, is strongly republican and anti-authoritarian. In American literature, until recently, most writers have reflected the democratic traditions of their country and have been angrily conscious of the increasing encroachments by vested interests. The American novel particularly met these encroachments with a call to resistance—Norris, London, Howells, Dreiser, Upton Sinclair, Sinclair Lewis, Steinbeck, and others. In the thirties, because of the still-fresh memories of the Hoover years, and the tendencies of the New Deal, the content of the novel (and of what drama and poetry there was) was left of center. What an ideological gap divides the poems and novels of the Southern Agrarians from Whitman and Sandburg, and from Norris and Dreiser!

The first point of attack then of the New Criticism, if reactionary views were to be popularized, was to establish the general thesis that the content of literature is not important in literary evaluation. This objective was partly achieved by concentrating critical attention on the literature "itself," which meant, in practice, an analysis of forms and techniques. From one aspect, this concern with, say, the poem itself was beneficial; it became pernicious where, in a final estimate, it ignored consideration of what the poem says. In this sense, these critics were "New" in that they flouted all the traditions of the previous centuries. That a piece of writing is a form of communication between author and audience is, in fact, the only conception that any eighteenth- or nineteenth-century critic would recognize.

The practical upshot of this new theory is a pseudo-impartiality which evades any choice between good and evil. Good and evil may be considered as religious, philosophical, political, moral, or literary values. These values are intrinsic in literature as they are intrinsic in life itself. The real aim of the New Critics in shunting away attention from the ideas of literature, that is, from life, has been clearly expressed by Robert Heilman, who holds with this caucus. Robert Gorham Davis charged that Heilman, in the *Sewanee Review,* "contended that holding liberal-democratic-progressive views with any conviction made one incapable of approaching imaginative literature at all." [22] Well might we ask: does the converse also obtain?

The chieftains and clansmen of the New Criticism agree to the divorce of content and form, and consider communication and subject matter unimportant. Thus Ransom discusses the "poetry of things" and "the poetry of ideas," and dismisses the latter as Platonic and Victorian. He praises the Imagists as

> . . . important figures in the history of our poetry, and they were both theorists and creators. It was their in-

tention to present things in their thinginess, or *Dinge* in their *Dinglichkeit*; and to such an extent had the public lost its sense of *Dinglichkeit* that their re-direction was wholesome. What the public was inclined to seek in poetry was ideas, whether large ones or small ones, grand ones or pretty ones, certainly ideas to live by and die by, but what the Imagists identified with the stuff of poetry was, simply, things.[23]

Allen Tate makes a similar argument:

I am attacking here the fallacy of communication in poetry. It is no less a fallacy of composition than of criticism. The critical doctrine fares ill the further back you apply it; I suppose one may say—if one wants a landmark—that it began to prosper after 1798; for on the whole nineteenth-century English verse is a poetry of communication. The poets were trying to use verse to convey ideas and feelings that they thought secretly could be better conveyed by science (consult Shelley's *Defense*), or by what today we call, in a significantly bad poetic phrase, the Social Sciences. Yet for some reason, possibly because the poets believed the scientists to be tough, and the scientists thought the poets tender, the poets stuck to verse. If that is a bad near tradition, it may hardly be said that we change it by giving it a new name, by giving it another brand of patriotism.[24]

It might be noted that in this essay Tate condemns Edna St. Vincent Millay's "Justice Denied in Massachusetts," a simple poem, liberal in sentiment, as "impenetrably obscure," while exalting Pound's involved, difficult, and pro-fascist Cantos, as "distinguished verse."

Brooks, discussing Wordsworth's "Westminster Bridge," says the same in slightly different words:

> The attempt to account for it on the grounds of nobility of sentiment soon breaks down. On this level, the poem merely says: that the city in the morning light presents a picture which is majestic and touching to all but the most dull of soul; but the poem says very little more about the sight: the city is beautiful in the morning light and it is awfully still. The attempt to make a case for the poem in terms of the brilliance of its images also quickly breaks down.[25]

How similar these statements are to those of the master, writing, for example, about "The Social Function of Poetry":

> The other type of bad poet is not a virtuoso; he has found a serious purpose; he has a message to convey. This type of bad poet is apt to run to very long poems, even to the epic. He usually keeps to a well-tried vocabulary and long approved metre; he aims at the sublime rather than the eccentric. He has a religious, or a philosophical, or a political turn of mind; and his poetry is the vehicle of a message which he is sure is of importance to the world. He has a social purpose; and he has nothing else.[26]

In spite of this contempt for meaning, Eliot on a few occasions, and for a limited audience, allows that poetry without meaning is not good poetry. In the privately printed pamphlet circulated by Messrs Harcourt Brace, Eliot in 1948 showed flashes of that acumen which had originally brought him to critical attention:

> Poetry, of different kinds, may be said to range from
> that in which the attention of the reader is directed
> primarily to the sound, to that in which it is directed
> primarily to the sense. With the former kind, the sense
> may be apprehended almost unconsciously; with the
> latter kind—at these two extremes—it is the sound, of
> the operation of which upon us we are unconscious.
> But, with either type, sound and sense must cooperate;
> in even the most purely incantatory poem, the diction-
> ary meaning of words cannot be disregarded with im-
> punity.[27]

Having denied the unity of content and form, and distracted attention from the meaning, the way is now open
for the second stage of the New Criticism program. Under
the subterfuge that meaning is secondary, the critics begin
to praise poetry or prose which has a strongly conservative
content and to damn all literature that is even slightly humanist. The reader is obviously receiving some communication—even if vague and mystic—but, because he has been
told meaning is unimportant, tends consciously to disregard
what he is reading. Subconsciously, while spending considerable time analyzing any work for style, he is accepting
its reactionary ideas. Thus implicitly, or even explicitly,
fascist material gains attention, allegedly as literature.

Allen Tate opened the *Southern Review* with such a
façade of impartiality. On debatable topics he implied some
variety by his contributors: "The editor may not believe in
Marxism, but he will see it as an issue, and he will seek discussion of Marxism from a point of view." [28] What that
point of view is and what little room it provided for debate

may be seen in the fourth volume where Sidney Hook offers anti-Communist "Reflections on the Russian Revolution" (pp. 429-462); Henry B. Parkes notes "Some Marxist Fallacies" (pp. 474-488), and Philip Rahv discusses "Proletarian Literature: A Political Autopsy" (pp. 616-628).

Eliot likewise professed the broad, open-minded approach and avoidance of partisan politics. Writing a commendatory letter to a new periodical, *The Catacomb,* for the Summer of 1950, Eliot said: "For some years literature was involved with a silly kind of political enthusiasm. Less is heard about that now, in fact I think it is generally the opinion that the less said about politics the better, and that a literary review should disclose no convictions." [29] His own *The Criterion* had started out with similarly disarming professions: it was to be open to all points of view. But the editorials took on a very one-sided aspect, under the typical alibi of presenting both sides of the question. So we find wary praises of fascism and the new British fascist movement led by Sir Oswald Mosley: "The Mosley programme (Macmillan: 6d.), though in some respects vague or feeble, contains at least some germs of intelligence, and a pronouncement by men who have had the courage to disassociate themselves from any party must be read with respect. It recognises that the nineteenth century is over, and that a thorough reorganization of industry and of agriculture is essential." [30]

The Southern scholars have fastened an octopus hold on the American academic and literary world. Their doctrines have been spread by the "little" magazines of which they have gained control. Among the earlier journals were *Hound and Horn,* edited by Blackmur (1927-1934), which had Tate as its Southern editor (1929-1932); and *The Fugitive,* at first printing only poetry, founded and edited by Ransom (1922-1925), coedited by Tate (1922-1925), and joined by Warren (1924). After these magazines came *Southern Review,* jointly edited by Brooks (1935-1942) and Warren, with Eliot as advisory editor; the long-established *Sewanee Review* under the editorship of Tate (1944-1946); and the *Kenyon Review,* founded and edited by Ransom in 1939, with Warren (1942) and Tate (1939-1942) as advisory editors.

A quartet, Ransom, Tate, Brooks, and Warren, has thus dominated the critical scene for the past twenty years. Their influence proved so pervasive that it swayed later journals, such as the *Hudson Review* (to which *Hound and Horn* Blackmur is a contributor). Wherever a young intellectual looked, and he would naturally look to the aesthetic magazines for escape from the limited and limiting Main Street standards of American Life, he was confronted by southern Agrarianism. And while Ransom and Tate might be his meat, the younger college student would have his literary diet provided by Brooks and Warren, whose jointly written textbooks, *Understanding Poetry* (1938), *An Approach to Literature* (1941), and *Understanding Fiction* (1943), have had a wide acceptance.

The power of this group was demonstrated in the award to Ezra Pound of the Bollingen prize. It was absurd, observed the *Saturday Review of Literature* editorially, to claim the award as "entirely non-political." [31] Most American intellectuals had known of the cantos of Pound with their occasional powerful images, and their similarity to Eliot in the use of the technique of recall. (That this technique frequently made no sense—where Pound strung together catenas of misquoted quotations—has been amply demonstrated.[32]) They had known that Pound had been revolted by the superficialities and shams of post-War I America, and had lived as an expatriate in France and Italy. But they had known also that Pound was an admirer of Italian fascism and had rendered service to Mussolini all during the time the United States was at war with Italy. Brought back to America and indicted as a fascist traitor, he escaped a formal trial by pleading insanity. This was the person to whom the Fellows of the Library of Congress presented the Bollingen Award, for the most outstanding volume of verse *published during 1948.* The award was not made for Pound's early poems.

Public shock at this award, which traduced American literary accomplishment and literary criticism before world opinion, found its strongest expression in Robert Hillyer's two articles in the *Saturday Review of Literature.* He charged that the Fellows were dominated by an Eliot—New Critics clique.[33] In reply, the individuals concerned and *Poetry* Magazine accused Hillyer of ill-temper. But his charge remained unanswered. Eliot and the Southern Agrarians among the Fellows had voted solidly for Pound. The Eliot group had thus declared to the world that in their opinion (because of the associations of the award, a semi-official opinion) the greatest American poet in 1948 was a fascist and/or a madman.

Just as the content of Pound's verses is carefully avoided on typical New Criticism grounds, so it is that in all the many discussions of the magnitude of Eliot as a writer, there is seldom any discussion of what he says. Fully aware that the content or subject matter is of importance in literary creation, Allen Tate skillfully tries to disqualify *a priori* all those who refuse to disregard the content of Eliot's later work by saying: "The reasoning that is being brought to bear upon Mr. Eliot's recent verses is as follows: Anglo-Catholicism would not at all satisfy me; therefore, his poetry declines under its influence." [34] It is surprising that such a scholar as F. O. Matthiessen swallowed the bait. The converse, it might be pointed out to Mr. Tate, is equally invalid: "The political and social aspects of Eliot's interpretation of Anglo-Catholicism satisfy me; therefore his poetry improves under their influence."

This resolute blindness to meaning reaches grotesque lengths. If we come across a piece of anti-Semitic writing, our immediate reaction is that this is filth. But how do the critics treat Eliot's anti-Semitic "Gerontion"? Wolf Mankowitz, in his discussion of the poem, omits "And the jew (sic) squats on the window sill . . ." and starts his quotation at

> the owner
> Spawned in some estaminet of Antwerp. . . .
> Blistered in Brussels, patched and peeled in London. . . .

Ignoring the key word "jew," Dr. Mankowitz unconcernedly interprets "the owner": " 'Spawned' in its associations with the breeding of the lower animals, suggests a repulsive promiscuous sexuality, a teeming like the Egyptian plague; while 'blistered,' 'patched' and 'peeled' in conjunction with 'estaminet' imply the diseased debasement of brothels." [35] On the other early poems, Frank Wilson merely finds in the description of Bleistein "an accumulation of sordid epithet undistinguished by any great energy. This too-laboured description of Bleistein. . . ." [36] Again, no acknowledgment that the description is anti-Semitic. Mr. Wilson, however, later edits Eliot's line to "the Jew [capital letter] is underneath the lot," and finds a parallel in Byron. Matthiessen does not mention the line, and McGreevy omits the lines which are anti-Semitic.[37] Two other comments on "Burbank with a Baedeker; Bleistein with a Cigar" may be quoted. Dr. Hyatt Howe Waggoner analyzes how Eliot intensifies his anti-Semitism in his picture of Bleistein:

> "Another device besides anti-Semitism is here used to make the character repulsive: Bleistein's eyes are not only lustreless and protrusive but they stare 'from the protozoic slime.' The evolutionary movement is reversed in the description of Bleistein to make him at once repellent and modern." [38]

The most outspoken discussion of Eliot's anti-Semitism is perhaps that made by Robert Graves, who observes that Bleistein is "a caricature Jew" and "a symbol of vulgar and ignorant self-enjoyment." Graves continues:

> Burbank sees the strength and wealth of Venice departed, the remnants of her glory enjoyed by an upstart Chicago Jew who probably started life as a furrier's apprentice in Leopoldstadt, the Jewish quarter of Vienna. . . . Burbank sorrowfully pictures the Rialto

of other days. The rats are underneath the piles now,
and the Jew (the eternal Shylock) is the rat of rats.
The jew (Jew is written with a small initial letter like
rat) is a rat because he has made money and because
for some reason Jewish wealth, as opposed to Gentile
wealth, has a mystical connexion with the decline of
Venice. This may not be Burbank's private opinion,
or even Mr. Eliot's. It at any rate expresses for Burbank and Mr. Eliot the way Venice at present feels, or
should feel, about the modern Jew strutting through
her streets.[39]

Critics have vied with each other to prove Eliot the great
writer. They have twisted the meaning and in their idola-
try have even misread the words Eliot wrote. Every word is
interpreted, expanded, eulogized. A single line, sometimes a
single word, furnishes the basis for a prolonged commentary. In the Third Section of *The Waste Land,* Eliot describes the return of a typist to her lodgings; she

> clears her breakfast, lights
> Her stove, and lays out food in tins.
> Out of the window perilously spread
> Her drying combinations touched by the sun's
> last rays,
> On the divan are piled (at night her bed)
> Stockings, slippers, camisoles, and stays.

But the words of Eliot are not sufficient for the critics.
To Matthiessen, the "divan" transcends the studio couch of
thousands of furnished rooms in London and New York:
"So, too, the word 'divan' raises all its glamorous connotations from the Orient, which are instantly broken into by

the realization that this is the kind of perfected folding divan that can be bought at a bargain at Selfridge's or Macy's,
and which is designed to do double work." [40]

Proceeding further, Matthiessen finds a grammatical nu-
ance. To Eliot he needlessly imputes a freedom from ordinary rules of syntax. In this he disagrees with a critic in
The Dublin Review, who, having complained of Eliot's
"false and muddled grammar of sense and syntax," comments that the following lines are "a marvellous creation of
baffling hotch-potch." [41]

> At the violet hour, the evening hour that strives
> Homeward, and brings the sailor home from sea,
> The typist home at teatime, clears her breakfast. . . .

Matthiessen comments:

> The limpid description of the evening, with its roman-
> tic associations heightened by the echo of Stevenson's
> 'Requiem' as well as by the emulation of some lines of
> Sappho (of which Eliot tells us in a note), is suddenly
> startled into a new aspect by the appearance of the typ-
> ist. It is worth observing that this effect of surprise is
> made partly by the equally sudden shift in syntax,
> whereby 'the typist', at first the object of 'brings,' be-
> comes in turn the subject of 'clears.' [42]

There is no need for so recherché an explanation: the
lines are reasonably straightforward: "the evening hour" is
grammatically an appositive to "the violet hour"; "typist" is
the object of the verb "can see" (in the preceding lines:

"I Tiresias . . . can see . . . the typist"). Eliot has simply omitted the relative pronoun "who" ("The typist [who] clears her breakfast"). And if any comment were needed, it should suffice to point out that as the imagery is impressionistic, so is the syntax fluid and impressionistic.

This annotation approaches the ludicrous in the fantastic mélange of adolescent purple patches and inflated rhetoric in *T. S. Eliot and the Lay Reader* by E. M. Stephenson. Commenting on two lines in *The Dry Salvages*

> And right action is freedom
> From past and future also

Miss Stephenson writes: "For pure interest it is worth noting that a similar phrase comes from Erigena, a mystical philosopher of pre-scholastic times, whom Mr. Eliot tells me he has never read—'Authority comes from right reason.' " [43]

So too a critic has been known to rewrite Eliot's own words. Dr. Wolf Mankowitz, again, discussing the words "weeds flourish" in "Gerontion", makes this note: "The highly conscious selection of the weed 'dogweed,' anticipates Mr. Eliot's later use of the Dog archetype in *The Waste Land* and "Marina." [44] The effect here is the clear definition of the 'weeds.' " But, by misreading "dogwood" as "dogweed," Mankowitz has ignored the beautiful flowering tree with bright white or pink blossoms in May and has invented what he seems to imagine as a kind of stinkweed. Dr. Mankowitz could have avoided this blunder had he realized that the line itself was not original, but taken from *The Education of Henry Adams.* So Anne Ridler also rewrites Eliot, misquoting "hooves" instead of "heels" from the "Triumphal March." [45]

The Eliot problem, then, is largely the problem of the *critics* of Eliot. Reactionary critics welcome him because of his own reactionary position, though they claim to be governed by objective aesthetic criteria. Other critics, attracted by his skill but disturbed by his reactionary thinking, ignore its significance or edit away its more offensive evidences.

In both cases there is an evasion of the larger problem out of which the Eliot problem arises—how the writer functions in society. In certain ways the writer is more aware of the world and those who live in it than the rest of us. This awareness gives him something particular to say to us—incites his urge to write and gives value to what he has to say. At the same time, he has also the responsibility to report the truth and to communicate clearly.

Since the world has never yet known perfection, part of the writer's awareness has been critical—the recognition and report of the imperfections. That is why the mainstream tradition of literature has been critical and why writers of consequence have so often been on the side of protest and insurgency. But that is also why writers whose work distracted attention from the imperfections gained official favor—not only prizes and emoluments but every service calculated to enhance their prestige and enlarge their audience.

Our time is no different. Its imperfections are tragically

obvious—scarcity where plenty is possible, an increasing absorption of productive capacity for destructive ends, a shackling of thought, and calls for a moratorium on science just when the horizons of knowledge have opened wider and conditions have become more favorable for extending intellectual opportunity. A contemporary writer, consequently, has as much occasion for a critical report as writers of any previous period.

In our time, too, the powerful and entrenched—and we have seen how even the non-commercial literary journals have passed into the hands of their literary allies—have awarded their favors to those writers and schools which help divert attention from troubling realities. The various cults of mysticism and irrationality, the Yogi-Vedanta searchings (of writers like Gerald Heard, Aldous Huxley, and Christopher Isherwood), the imported Existentialists, the "tough" writers who offer release in brute action freed from the disciplines and responsibilities of thinking, have received a "good press."

These trends are especially noticeable in those countries which have not had first-hand experience of the workings of fascism.[46] Nor is this really surprising; it is not sufficiently understood how useful are the *literary* cults of mysticism, irrationality, and violence to fascist political tendencies, which themselves rely heavily on *political* mysticism, irrationality, and violence. In so far as any writer presents such concepts in a favorable light, he is promoting their widespread diffusion.

The current Eliot vogue is no mystery; the Eliot problem no enigma: it is the logical reflection of present-day decadence. Those who shrug off, or are themselves caught up in, this trend should at least realize what they are heading toward: the suppression of all creative activities, ultimately including their own, and the abandonment of the mainstream tradition of culture and enlightenment.

FOOTNOTES

1. Chapters or passages which from various standpoints are critical of some aspect of Eliot's work are found in the following: H. W. Garrod, *Genius Loci and Other Essays* (Oxford, 1950); Robert Graves, *The Common Asphodel* (London, 1949); Harold J. Laski, *Faith, Reason, and Civilization* (New York, 1944); C. S. Lewis, *Rehabilitation* (London, 1939); E. M. W. Tillyard, *Poetry Direct and Oblique* (London, 1945); Rosamund Tuve, *Elizabethan and Metaphysical Imagery* (Chicago, 1947); Hyatt H. Waggoner, *The Heel of Elohim* (Norman, 1950); Yvor Winters, *The Anatomy of Nonsense* (New York, 1943), *Primitivism and Decadence* (New York, 1937).

2. Ernest S. Bates, "T. S. Eliot: Leisure Class Laureate," *The Modern Quarterly* (Baltimore), VII (February, 1933), pp. 17-24; L. A. Cormican, "Mr. Eliot and Social Biology," *Scrutiny,* XVII (Spring, 1950), pp. 2-13; Robert G. Davis, "The New Criticism and the Democratic Tradition," *American*

Scholar, XIX (Winter, 1949), pp. 9-19; Robert Hillyer, "Poetry's New Priesthood," *The Saturday Review of Literature,* June 18, 1949, pp. 7-9, 38; R. H. Hinton, "Culture and T. S. Eliot," *Modern Quarterly* (London), VI (Spring, 1951), pp. 147-162; D. S. Mirsky, *"T. S. Eliot et la fin de la poésie bourgeoisée,"* *Echanges* (Décembre, 1931), pp. 44-58; Harold U. Ribalow, "T. S. Eliot—Poet and Prejudice," *Congress Weekly,* November 15, 1948, pp. 7-8; Rossell Hope Robbins, "The T. S. Eliot Myth," *Science and Society,* XIV (Winter, 1949-50), pp. 1-28; S. J. Wyndham, "Outline for a Critical Approach to T. S. Eliot," *Contemporary Issues* (London), I (Winter, 1948), pp. 106-116.

3. Robert W. Stallman, *Critiques and Essays in Criticism 1920-48* (New York, 1949), p. 510.

4. James Reeves, "Cambridge Twenty Years Ago," in *T. S. Eliot: A Symposium,* ed. Richard March and Tambimuttu (London, 1948), p. 42.

5. Richard Lea, "T. S. Eliot's Four Quartets," *The Adelphi,* XXI (July, 1945), p. 186.

6. Leonard Unger, *T. S. Eliot: A Selected Critique* (New York, 1948), p. xi.

7. Joseph Wood Krutch, "T. S. Eliot on Broadway," *New York Herald Tribune,* Book Review Section, March 19, 1950.

8. M[uriel] C. Bradbrook, *T. S. Eliot* (The British Council: London, 1950), p. 52.

9. *Time,* Vol. IV, No. 10 (March 6, 1950).

10. Michael F. Maloney, "Mr. Eliot and Critical Tradition," *Thought,* XXI (September, 1946), p. 474.

11. Elizabeth Vassifieff, "Piers to Cocktails," *Meanjin* (Victoria), IX (Spring, 1950), pp. 193-203.

12. Eliot, in his Introduction to Ezra Pound's *Selected Poems* (London, 1928), p. viii, says his early verse "was di-

rectly drawn from the study of Laforgue together with the late Elizabethan drama." René Taupin has made several detailed studies, *e.g., L'Influence du symbolisme français sur la poésie américaine* (Paris, 1929); "The Classicism of T. S. Eliot," *The Symposium,* III (January, 1932), pp. 64-81. See also E. J. H. Greene, "Jules Laforgue et T. S. Eliot," *Revue de Littérature Comparée,* XXII (1948), pp. 363-397.

13. Introduction to Ezra Pound, *Selected Poems* (London, 1928), p. viii.

14. "The Function of Criticism," *Selected Essays (1917-1932)* (New York, 1932), p. 21.

15. "John Marston," *Selected Essays* (London, 1949), p. 233.

16. "Donne in Our Time," in *A Garland for John Donne,* ed. Theodore Spencer (Cambridge, Mass., 1931), p. 12.

17. New York *Daily Mirror,* January 23, 1950.

18. I. A. Richards, quoted by Eliot in *The Use of Poetry* (London, 1948), p. 17.

19. "The Possibility of a Poetic Drama," *The Sacred Wood* (London, 1948), p. 64.

20. "Religion and Literature," *Essays Ancient and Modern* (London, 1936), p. 93.

21. *Ibid.,* p. 94.

22. *Christian News Letter,* No. 97 (September 3, 1941).

23. *Ibid.*

24. Saul K. Padover, *Democracy by Thomas Jefferson* (New York, 1939), p. 32.

25. *Christian News Letter,* No. 97 (September 3, 1941).

26. *The Criterion,* VIII (December, 1928), p. 288. H. O. Pappe, in "Some Notes on Mr. Eliot's Culture," *Landfall* (Dunedin), IV (September, 1950), p. 240, points out further the meaning of Eliot's treatment of Maurras: "One of the few con-

temporaries who are quoted in a friendly vein by Mr. Eliot, and
from whose spiritual world he seems to derive much of his attitude, is Charles Maurras. Like Mr. Eliot, Maurras grew up in
the world of the Greeks and Dante. But has this made him fit
to meet the challenge of contemporary history? His politics, as
D. W. Brogan (*French Personalities and Problems*) has termed
it, are the politics of hate, and 'there is only hate.' He has been
connected with nearly everthing despicable in modern Europe—
as the hater of Weimar Germany's tender democratic leanings,
and the vilifier of Keyne's call for European reconciliation; as
the admirer and collaborator of Hitler's Germany, the hater of
the 'twice barbarous' Anglo-Saxon way of life (twice barbarous
because individualist and liberal); the instigator of attempted
political murder (Leon Blum's, for which he was sent to
prison); the upholder of injustice on principle, and of perjury.
His classical education, and his consciousness of superiority did
not protect him, as little as they protected il miglior fabbro, Mr.
Eliot's friend Ezra Pound, the admirer and collaborator of
Mussolini. This is not to suggest that Mr. Eliot approves of their
aberrations. But he is gentle and understanding with them,
while he is strict and sarcastic towards others whose moral record is *not* blemished. When it is a matter of attacking Harold
Laski, a newspaper sentence torn from its context is good
enough. Yet Laski has clearly stated his views in books (if
anything too often)."

27. *The Criterion,* VIII (December, 1928), p. 290.

28. Alfred Kazin, *On Native Ground* (New York, 1942),
p. 428.

29. *After Strange Gods* (London, 1934), p. 16.

30. *The Criterion,* X (April, 1932), p. 483.

31. *Notes towards the Definition of Culture* (New York,
1949), p. 27.

32. *Ibid.,* p. 74.

33. Robert Hillyer, "Treason's Strange Fruit," *The Saturday Review of Literature*, June 11, 1949, p. 28.

34. For example, *The Idea of a Christian Society*, Brussels, 1946; *After Strange Gods*, Oslo, 1948.

35. *Christian News Letter*, No. 97 (September 3, 1941).

36. *The Criterion*, X (July, 1932), p. 771.

37. "Modern Education and the Classics," *Essays Ancient and Modern,* p. 161.

38. *Notes towards the Definition of Culture*, pp. 103-104.

39. *Ibid.,* p. 105. This idea had been noted as "totalitarianism" by Eliot in 1939 in *The Idea of a Christian Society* (New York, 1940), p. 83.

40. "Lambeth and Education: The Report Criticized," *The Guardian*, No. 5441 (April 6, 1950), pp. 310, 311.

41. *Ibid.*

42. Eliot has tried to backtrack from his dogmatism in an interview with Foster Hailey in the *New York Sunday Times* (April 16, 1950): "Some people want to get a general statement on marriage out of the relations of Edward and Lavinia. You can't depict all of your views about life. You are limited by time."

43. *The Idea of a Christian Society* (London, 1939), p. 62.

44. *The Criterion*, XIV (April, 1935), p. 433.

45. *After Strange Gods*, p. 20.

46. *The Idea of a Christian Society*, pp. 35-36.

47. Eliot, although he had lived so much of his life in America, prints this word with a small *n* in *The Criterion*, XV (January, 1936), p. 267. In *Four Quartets,* however, he uses a capital *N* (*The Dry Salvages*, II).

48. *The New English Weekly*, XVI (February 15, 1940), p. 251.

49. *Notes towards the Definition of Culture,* p. 110.

50. *After Strange Gods,* p. 16.

51. Peter Russell, "A Note on T. S. Eliot's New Play," *Nine,* I (Autumn, 1949), p. 29.

52. "Thoughts after Lambeth," *Selected Essays* (New York, 1932), p. 332.

53. "Second Thoughts about Humanism," *Selected Essays,* p. 402.

54. "Thoughts after Lambeth," *Selected Essays,* p. 314.

55. *After Strange Gods,* p. 57.

56. John Baillie and Hugh Martin, *Revelation* (London, 1937), p. 38.

57. *Ibid.,* p. 2. Although this division is "the most profound," Eliot on the same page writes: "The line to be drawn between the Christian and the non-Christian world is at present extremely difficult to draw."

58. In *After Strange Gods,* in 1934, Eliot was publicly saying, "I speak as a New Englander" (p. 16) and calling himself "a Yankee" (p. 20). In 1928, after he had become a British subject, he was saying, "I myself had always been a New Englander in the South West, and a South Westerner in New England"—preface, p. xiii, to Edgar Ansell Mowrer, *This American World* (London, 1928).

59. H. V. Routh in *The Year's Work in English Studies,* XXVIII (1947), p. 255.

NOTES TO CHAPTER TWO

1. M. C. Bradbrook, "Eliot's Critical Method," in *T. S. Eliot: A Study of his Writings by Several Hands,* ed. B. Rajan (*Focus* III) (London, 1947), p. 122.

2. John Hayward has dated the poems in Pierre Leyris' French translation of Eliot, *Poèmes 1910-1930* (Paris, 1947). In an article on Ezra Pound in *Poetry,* LXVIII (April-September, 1946), p. 327, Eliot says: "I had kept my early poems (including *Prufrock* and others eventually published) in my desk from 1911 to 1915."

3. *Harvard Advocate,* CXXV (December, 1938), p. 16.

4. Louis MacNeice, "Eliot and the Adolescent," in *T. S. Eliot: A Symposium,* ed. Richard March and Tambimuttu (London, 1948), pp. 150-151.

5. *The Idea of a Christian Society* (New York, 1940) p. 17.

6. "Modern Education and the Classics," *Essays Ancient and Modern* (London, 1936), p. 161.

7. Leonard Unger, *T. S. Eliot: A Selected Critique* (New York, 1948), p. xix.

8. "Thoughts after Lambeth," *Selected Essays* (New York, 1932), p. 314.

9. Cleanth Brooks, *Modern Poetry and the Tradition* (London, 1948), p. 137.

10. "Shakespeare and the Stoicism of Seneca," *Selected Essays,* p. 108.

11. "The Social Function of Poetry" (1943 version), *The Norseman,* I (November, 1943), p. 449.

12. The Essay on Marston was written in 1934 although the essays were still advertised as 1917-1932. The title page in the last edition is, however, without dates.

13. "John Bramhall," *Selected Essays,* p. 302.

14. *After Strange Gods* (London, 1934), p. 12.

15. *The Idea of a Christian Society,* p. 24.

16. *Notes towards the Definition of Culture* (New York, 1949), p. 11.

17. *Ibid.,* p. 88

18. *The Idea of a Christian Society*, p. 3.

19. *The New English Weekly*, XVI (February 8, 1940), p. 237.

20. *The Idea of a Christian Society*, p. 61.

21. *Notes towards the Definition of Culture*, p. 93.

22. *Ibid.*, p. 59.

23. The Idea of a Christian Society, pp. 70-71.

24. "Thoughts after Lambeth," p. 332.

25. *Notes towards the Definition of Culture*, p. 102.

26. *Ibid.*, p. 32.

27. "A Dialogue on Dramatic Poetry," *Selected Essays*, p. 44.

28. "The Aims of Poetic Drama," [The Poets' Theatre Guild, London] (1949), p. 5.

29. "Catholicism and International Order," *Essays Ancient and Modern*, p. 130.

30. *After Strange Gods*, p. 13.

31. *The Idea of a Christian Society*, p. 50.

32. *Ibid.*, p. 23.

33. *Ibid.*, p. 39.

34. *Ibid.*, pp. 6-7.

35. "Second Thoughts about Humanism," *Selected Essays*, p. 397.

36. "Religion and Literature," *Essays Ancient and Modern*, p. 108.

37. "Catholicism and International Order," p. 120.

38. "In Memoriam," *Essays Ancient and Modern*, p. 187.

39. *The Idea of a Christian Society*, p. 10.

40. "Modern Education and the Classics," *Essays Ancient and Modern*, p. 172.

41. *Notes towards the Definition of Culture*, p. 74.

42. *Ibid.*, p. 73.

43. New York *Daily News*, January 23, 1950.

44. *After Strange Gods*, p. 16.

45. *The New English Weekly*, VIII (September 12, 1935), p. 351.

46. John Strachey, *The Coming Struggle for Power* (New York, rev. ed. 1934), p. 221.

47. *The Idea of a Christian Society*, p. 95.

48. *Ibid.*, p. 98.

49. *Ibid.*, p. 51.

50. "Catholicism and International Order," p. 114.

51. *Ibid.*

52. *The Idea of a Christian Society*, p. 47.

53. "Catholicism and International Order," p. 129.

54. *The Idea of a Christian Society*, p. 96.

55. *Ibid.*, p. 51.

56. "Catholicism and International Order," pp. 123-124.

57. *The Idea of a Christian Society*, p. 34.

58. *Ibid.*, pp. 35-36.

59. *After Strange Gods*, p. 20.

60. "Religion and Literature," p. 100.

61. "Catholicism and International Order," pp. 113-114.

62. "Thoughts after Lambeth," p. 365.

63. *Ibid.*, p. 356.

64. *The Idea of a Christian Society*, p. 48.

65. "Catholicism and International Order," p. 131.

66. *The New English Weekly*, XVIII (December 5, 1940), p. 69.

67. *The Idea of a Christian Society*, p. 61.

68. *Ibid.*, p. 35.

69. *Ibid.*, p. 61.

70. *Notes towards the Definition of Culture*, p. 74.

71. *Ibid.*, p. 75.

72. *Ibid.*, p. 83.

73. *The New English Weekly,* XVI (December 7, 1939), p. 8.

74. *Notes towards the Definition of Culture,* p. 17.

75. *The New English Weekly,* XVI (February 8, 1940), p. 238.

76. P. B. and E. M. W. Tillyard, *Milton: Private Correspondence and Academic Exercises* (Cambridge, 1932), p. 112.

77. *The Criterion,* X (January, 1925), p. 280.

78. *Ibid.,* VII (February, 1928), p. 98.

79. *The Idea of a Christian Society,* p. 17.

80. *Ibid.,* p. 69.

81. Simon Haxly, *Tory M. P.* (London, 1939), pp. 207-209.

82. *The Criterion,* XVI (March, 1937), p. 473.

83. *Ibid.,* XVI (July, 1937), p. 669.

84. *The Idea of a Christian Society,* p. 17.

85. *Ibid.,* p. 70.

86. *Ibid.*

87. *Ibid.,* pp. 5-6.

88. *Ibid.,* pp. 15-16.

89. *Ibid.,* p. 18.

90. *Manchester Guardian,* August 24, 1949.

91. *The Idea of a Christian Society,* p. 31.

92. *Ibid.,* p. 7.

93. *Notes towards the Definition of Culture,* p. 17.

94. *Ibid.,* p. 18.

95. *Ibid.,* pp. 84-85.

96. *The Criterion,* VIII (October, 1928), p. 281.

97. *Notes towards the Definition of Culture,* p. 85.

98. *The Criterion,* VIII (October, 1928), p. 287.

99. *The New English Weekly,* XV (May 11, 1939), p. 61.

100. *The Criterion,* X (January, 1931), p. 309.

101. *Christian News Letter,* March 13, 1940, Supplement 20.

102. Two paragraphs (20 and 21) on education were omitted from the first chapter of the *Notes*; they continued the 1940 views and were in spirit behind parts of the sixth chapter: a warning against regarding education as "opportunity for the individual," and against the tendency to assume universal education necessarily good.

103. "Modern Education and the Classics," p. 164.

104. See above, footnote 53.

105. As reported in the *New York Times,* March 29, 1950.

106. Mr. Wallin "Voiced objections tonight in the 'widespread belief' that the government should provide an opportunity for higher education for all who desire it." *Ibid.*

107. *The Idea of a Christian Society,* p. 64.

108. *Notes towards the Definition of Culture,* p. 104.

109. *Ibid.,* p. 110.

110. *Ibid.,* p. 102.

111. "Baudelaire," *Selected Essays,* p. 339.

112. "Religion and Literature," p. 101.

113. "The Pensées of Pascal," *Essays Ancient and Modern,* p. 151, used as introduction for Everyman Library edition (London, 1948).

114. *After Strange Gods,* p. 34.

115. *Ibid.*

116. *The Idea of a Christian Society,* p. 8.

117. *Ibid.,* p. 40.

118. "Catholicism and International Order," p. 128.

119. Cf. Amy Nimr, "Introduction to the Poetry of Mr. T. S. Eliot," *Echanges,* No. 4 (Mars, 1931), p. 37: "He manipulates a whole paraphernalia of gloom."

120. *A Choice of Kipling's Verse* (London, 1941), p. 13.

121. "Religion and Literature," p. 100.

122. Francis J. Smith, "A Reading of 'East Coker,'" *Thought,* XXI (June, 1946), p. 286.

123. *Authors Take Sides* (London, 1937). Eliot explains his position in several editorials in *The Criterion,* e.g., XVI, pp. 289, which indicate little comprehension of the nature of the war.

124. William York Tindall, *Forces in Modern British Literature 1885-1946* (New York, 1947), p. 110.

NOTES TO CHAPTER THREE

1. *The Use of Poetry and The Use of Criticism* (London, 1948), p. 87.

2. *Ibid.,* p. 96.

3. *Ibid.,* p. 31.

4. *Old Possum's Book of Practical Cats* (New York, 1939), Helen Gardner, *The Art of T. S. Eliot* (London, 1949), p. 35, comments: "The brilliant dexterity of the verse . . . has hardly been recognized."

5. "Modern Education and the Classics," *Essays Ancient and Modern* (London, 1936), p. 172.

6. *The Use of Poetry,* p. 31.

7. Harold Laski, *Faith, Reason, and Civilization* (New York, 1944), p. 39.

8. *New York Herald Tribune,* Book Review Section, October 1, 1950.

9. Helen Gardner, *op. cit.,* p. 62.

10. *Ibid.*

11. "Thoughts after Lambeth," *Selected Essays* (New York, 1932), p. 316.

12. B. Rajan, "The Unity of the Quartets," in *T. S. Eliot: A Study of his Writings by Several Hands*, ed. B. Rajan (*Focus* III) (London, 1947), p. 94.

13. Raymond Preston, *"Four Quartets" Rehearsed* (London, 1946), p. 64.

14. *Murder in the Cathedral* (London, 1935), p. 48.

15. *After Strange Gods* (London, 1934), p. 21.

16. *Theology*, XLIV (February, 1942), p. 89. In 1950, when she was writing for the British Council, she softened her criticism: it "does in fact act extremely well" (p. 39).

17. E. Martin Browne, "The Dramatic Verse of T. S. Eliot," in *T. S. Eliot: A Symposium,* ed. Richard March and Tambimuttu (London, 1948), p. 202.

18. *After Strange Gods*, p. 42.

19. "John Marston," *Selected Essays* (London, 1949), p. 232.

20. Helen Gardner, *op. cit.,* p. 156.

21. Eliot in "Poetry and Drama," *The Atlantic,* Vol. 187, No. 2 (February, 1951), p. 36, says: "They must, in future, be omitted from the cast, and be understood to be visible only to certain of my characters, and not to the audience." Reprinted in book form (Cambridge, Mass., 1951).

22. "Thoughts after Lambeth," *Selected Essays* (New York, 1932), p. 319.

23. "Catholicism and International Order," *Essays Ancient and Modern*, p. 133.

24. *New York Times,* Book Review Section, March 19, 1950.

25. *The Use of Poetry*, p. 108.

26. *Milton* (London, 1948); also printed in *Proceedings of the British Academy*, XXXIII; and in *Sewanee Review*, LVI (Spring, 1948), pp. 185-209. James Holly Hanford, in the

New York Times, Book Review Section, November 6th, 1949, page 12, comments: "I think Eliot felt the need of recanting foolish ejaculation. But the recantation is external. Eliot hates Milton's guts. It's awfully silly, of course."

27. "A Note on the Verse of John Milton," *Essays and Studies by Members of the English Association,* XXI (Oxford; 1936), p. 33.

28. "Andrew Marvell," *Selected Essays,* p. 253.

29. "A Note on the Verse of John Milton," *loc. cit.,* p. 38. See further, *After Strange Gods,* p. 32: "it means very little to assert that if Milton had held more normal doctrines he would have written a better poem; as a work of literature, we take it as we find it: but we can certainly enjoy the poetry and yet be fully aware of the intellectual and moral aberrations of the author."

30. *The Use of Poetry,* p. 54.

31. "John Bramhall" *Essays Ancient and Modern,* p. 33.

32. *The Use of Poetry,* p. 106.

33. *Ibid.,* p. 89.

34. *Ibid.,* p. 96. In his Preface to Leone Vivante, *English Poetry* (New York, 1950), p. x, Eliot comments that he has been brought "to a new and more sympathetic appreciation" of Shelley.

35. "Marlowe," *Selected Essays,* p. 105.

36. *After Strange Gods,* p. 54.

37. Introduction to Ezra Pound, *Selected Poems* (London, 1928), p. xi.

38. *After Strange Gods,* p. 54.

39. "The Idea of a Literary Review," *The Criterion,* IV (July, 1926), p. 6.

40. *Ibid.*

41. *The Criterion,* XV (July, 1936), p. 708.

42. *A Choice of Kipling's Verse* (London, 1941), p. 25.

43. *The Idea of a Christian Society* (New York, 1940), p. vii.

44. *Ibid.*, p. 32.

45. *Notes towards the Definition of Culture* (New York, 1949), p. 31.

46. *The Idea of a Christian Society*, pp. 45-46.

47. *After Strange Gods*, p. 20.

48. "Catholicism and International Order," p. 133.

49. *Notes towards the Definition of Culture*, p. 16. Irwin Edman likened this work to "the meditations, often irascible and incoherent, of an educated English clergyman, possibly the head of a famous traditional public school, who was rather primly calling the world to order and reproving it for its nonsensical modern ideas, among them democracy." (*New York Times*, Book Review Section, March 6, 1949, page 22.)

50. L. A. Cormican, "Mr. Eliot and Social Biology," *Scrutiny*, XVII (Spring, 1950), p. 4.

51. *The New English Weekly*, XV (April, 1939), p. 28.

52. "The Social Function of Poetry" (1943 version), *The Norseman*, I (November, 1943), p. 453. The 1945 version, "Le Role social des poètes," an address given in Paris in May, 1945, was printed in English in *The Adelphi*, XXI (July, 1945), pp. 152-61; and reproduced by Robert W. Stallman. *Critiques and Essays in Criticism 1920-1948* (New York, 1949), pp. 105-116. The 1945 version shows some variants; here, for example: "We may say, then, that just as the first duty of a man *qua* citizen is to his country, so his first duty *qua* poet is to the language of his country. First, he has the duty to *preserve* that language: his use of it must not weaken, coarsen, or degrade it. Second, he has the duty to *develop* that language, to bring it

up to date, to investigate its unexplored possibilities." (*Loc. cit.*, p. 158.)

53. *The Use of Poetry*, p. 151.

54. *John O'London's Weekly,* quoted in *New York Times,* Book Review Section, September 11, 1949, p. 10.

55. Wilson Knight, *The Wheel of Fire* (Oxford, 1930), p. xiv.

56. *Scotsman*, August 23, 1949.

57. *Daily Telegraph,* August 24, 1949.

58. *News Chronicle,* August 27, 1949.

59. Cleanth Brooks, *Modern Poetry and the Tradition* (London, 1948), p. 146.

60. Frank Wilson, *Six Essays on the Development of T. S. Eliot* (London, 1948), p. 25.

61. Helen Gardner, *op. cit.,* p. 92.

62. *The Music of Poetry* (Glasgow, 1942), pp. 15-16.

63. Nevill Coghill, "*Sweeney Agonistes,*" in *T. S. Eliot: A Symposium*, ed. Richard March and Tambimuttu, p. 84.

64. *Ibid.,* p. 86.

65. *The Idea of a Christian Society*, p. 41.

66. *The New English Weekly,* VII (June 20, 1935), p. 190.

67. "Dante," *Selected Essays*, p. 217.

68. T. H. Thompson, "The Bloody Hand," *London Mercury*, XXIX (January, 1934), p. 238.

69. "Tradition and the Individual Talent," *Selected Essays*, p. 8.

70. *The Use of Poetry*, p. 22.

71. Wolf Mankowitz, "Notes on Gerontion," in *T. S. Eliot: A Study of his Writings by Several Hands,* ed. B. Rajan (*Focus* III), p. 138.

72. Helen Gardner, "*Four Quartets*: A Commentary," in *Focus* III, *op. cit.,* p. 57.

73. "Swinburne as Poet," *Selected Essays*, p. 284.

74. "Philip Massinger," *Selected Essays*, p. 182.

75. E. Allison Peers, *The Complete Works of Saint John of the Cross* (London, 1934), I, p. 63.

76. Quoted by Eliot in his essay on "Lancelot Andrewes," *Selected Essays*, p. 297.

77. Robert L. Morris, "Eliot's 'Game of Chess' and Conrad's 'The Return,'" *Modern Language Notes,* LXV (June, 1950), pp. 422-423.

78. William van O'Connor, "Gerontion and the Dream of Gerontius," *Furioso,* III (Winter, 1947), pp. 53-56.

79. Grover Smith, "T. S. Eliot and Sherlock Holmes," *Notes and Queries,* CXCIII (1948), pp. 431-432. The same point is made (without acknowledgment) by Alan Clutton-Brook, "T. S. Eliot and Conan Doyle," *The Times Literary Supplement,* January 19, 1951, p. 37.

80. "Poetry and Drama," *The Atlantic,* 187, No. 2 (February, 1950), p. 36.

81. Charles Williams, *Descent into Hell* (London, 1937), pp. 19, 47, 65, 93, 167.

82. Harold J. Laski, *Faith, Reason, and Civilization* (New York, 1944), p. 98.

83. E. M. W. Tillyard, *Poetry Direct and Oblique* (London, 1945), p. 33.

84. *Ibid.,* p. 34. F. O Matthiessen, *The Achievement of T. S. Eliot* (New York, 1947), p. 104, praises these lines: "where since Tourneur or Middleton has there been such bare sustained dramatic verse of the first order?"

85. Eliot does not make it clear whether Mary actually sees the Furies. See Note 21 above.

86. *The Family Reunion* (London, 1939), pp. 110, 147.

87. *Notes towards the Definition of Culture,* p. 29.

88. *The New English Weekly,* XVIII (December 5, 1940), p. 75.

89. *After Strange Gods,* p. 44.

90. "The Borderline of Prose," *New Statesman,* IX (May 19, 1917), p. 158.

91. *The Chapbook,* No. 22 (1921).

92. *Anabasis* (London, 1930), p. 8.

93. *The Use of Poetry,* p. 139.

94. Yvor Winters, *The Anatomy of Nonsense* (Norfolk, 1943), pp. 121-130. So also Delmore Schwartz, "The Literary Dictatorship of T. S. Eliot," *Partisan Review,* XVI (February, 1949), pp. 119-122.

95. Noted by Ernest S. Bates, "T. S. Eliot: Leisure Class Laureate," *The Modern Quarterly* (Baltimore), VII (February, 1933), p. 23.

96. "Blake," *The Sacred Wood* (London, 1948), p. 154.

97. *Ibid.,* pp. 157-158.

98. Bates, *loc. cit.,* p. 23.

99. "Imperfect Critics," *The Sacred Wood,* p. 17.

100. "The Social Function of Poetry" (1945 version), *loc. cit.,* p. 158.

101. Quoted by Matthiessen, *op. cit.,* p. 19.

102. "Shakespeare and the Stoicism of Seneca," *Selected Essays,* p. 117. Eliot, incidentally, expresses quite the contrary view in an editorial in *The Criterion,* XII, p. 77.

103. *The Idea of a Christian Society,* p. 20.

104. *A Choice of Kipling's Verse,* p. 7.

105. "The Social Function of Poetry" (1945 version), *loc. cit.,* p. 156.

106. "The Social Function of Poetry" (1943 version), *loc. cit.,* p. 454.

107. *The Sacred Wood,* p. vii.

108. *The Idea of a Christian Society,* p. 42.

109. "Modern Education and the Classics," p. 167.

110. *Notes towards the Definition of Culture,* p. 14.

111. *The Idea of a Christian Society,* p. 6.

112. *Ibid.,* p. 59.

113. *For Lancelot Andrewes* (London, 1928), p. ix.

114. *After Strange Gods,* pp. 27-28.

115. *Essays Ancient and Modern,* p. 5

116. *Horizon,* XII, No. 68 (August, 1945), p. 86.

NOTES TO CHAPTER FOUR

1. *After Strange Gods* (London, 1934), p. 52.

2. D. S. Mirsky, *"T. S. Eliot et la fin de la poésie bourgeoisée," Echanges* (Décembre, 1931), pp. 45-58. See also M. U. Schappes, "T. S. Eliot Moves Right," *Modern Monthly* (New York), VII (August, 1933), pp. 405-408.

3. *The Use of Poetry and the Use of Criticism* (London, 1948), p. 15.

4. *The Music of Poetry* (Glasgow, 1942), p. 13.

5. *New York Herald Tribune,* January 29, 1950.

6. *New York Times,* January 29, 1950.

7. "The Aims of Poetic Drama" [The Poets' Theatre Guild, London] (1949), pp. 5-6; partly reprinted as "T. S. Eliot on the Aims of Poetic Drama" in *New York Herald Tribune,* January 15, 1950.

8. When Eliot received his honorary degree at Oxford, this poem was recited (in Latin) by the University orator.

9. T. E. Hulme, *Speculations* (London, 1936), p. 52.

10. *Ibid.,* pp. 47-48.

11. "Second Thoughts about Humanism," *Hound and Horn,*

II (July-September, 1929), p. 349; reprinted in *Selected Essays* (New York, 1932), p. 401.

12. *The Criterion,* III (January, 1925), p. 280.

13. Herbert E. Palmer, "The Hoax and Earnest of *The Waste Land,*" *Dublin Review,* n.s., VIII (1933), p. 12.

14. R. B. Vance, *Southern Review,* I (1935-1936), p. 42.

15. Allen Tate, "The Function of the Critical Quarterly," *Southern Review,* I (1935-1936), p. 558.

16. "Mr. Eliot and Notions of Culture: A Discussion," *Partisan Review,* II (1944), p. 302.

17. *Ibid.,* p. 310.

18. *The Criterion,* X (April, 1931), p. 485.

19. "The Fallacy of Humanism," *Hound and Horn,* III (January-March, 1930), p. 255. The article was printed by Eliot in *The Criterion,* VIII (1929), pp. 660-681.

20. "A Traditionalist Looks at Liberalism," *Southern Review,* I (1935-1936), p. 737.

21. *Ibid.,* p. 739.

22. Robert B. Heilman, "Melpomene as Wallflower; or, The Reading of Tragedy," *Sewanee Review,* LV (Winter, 1947), pp. 154-166. Criticized by Robert Gorham Davis, "The New Criticism and The Democratic Tradition," *The American Scholar,* XIX (Winter, 1949), p. 10.

23. John Crowe Ransom, "Poetry: A Note in Ontology," *American Review,* III (May, 1934), pp. 173-174.

24. "Tension in Poetry," *The Southern Review,* IV (Summer, 1938), pp. 103-104.

25. "The Language of Paradox," in Allen Tate, *The Language of Poetry* (Princeton, 1942), pp. 39-40.

26. "The Social Function of Poetry" (1945 version), *The Adelphi,* XXI (July, 1945), p. 155.

27. *From Poe to Valery* (New York, 1948), p. 14.

28. *Southern Review,* I (1935-1936), p. 559.

29. *The Catacomb,* n.s., I (Summer, 1950).

30. *The Criterion,* X (April, 1932), p. 483.

31. "Ezra Pound and the Bollingen Award," *The Saturday Review of Literature,* June 11, 1949, pp. 20-21.

32. Margaret Schlauch, "The Anti-Humanism of Ezra Pound," *Science and Society,* XIII (Summer, 1949), pp. 258-269.

33. "Treason's Strange Fruit," *The Saturday Review of Literature,* June 11, 1949, pp. 9-11, 28; and "Poetry's New Priesthood," *ibid.,* June 18, 1949, pp. 7-9, 38.

34. *Hound and Horn,* IV January, (1931), p. 292; quoted by F. O. Matthiessen, *The Achievement of T. S. Eliot* (New York, 1947), p. 108.

35. Wolf Mankowitz, "Notes on Gerontion," in *Focus* III.

36. Frank Wilson, *Six Essays on the Development of T. S. Eliot* (London, 1948), p. 17.

37. Thomas McGreevy, *Thomas Stearns Eliot* (London, 1931), p. 58.

38. Hyatt Howe Waggoner, *The Heel of Elohim* (Norman, 1950), p. 79.

39. Robert Graves, *The Common Asphodel* (London, 1949), pp. 156-157.

40. Matthiessen, *op. cit.,* p. 31.

41. Herbert E. Palmer, *loc. cit.,* p. 15.

42. Matthiessen, *op. cit.,* p. 31.

43. E[llen] M[ary] Stephenson, *T. S. Eliot and the Lay Reader* (London, 1944), p. 22.

44. Wolf Mankowitz, "Notes on Gerontion," in *Focus* III, p. 132.

45. Anne Ridler, "A Question of Speech," in *Focus* III, p. 115.

46. In America, the admiration and influence of Eliot is far greater than it is in England, where adverse criticism is stronger. H. W. Garrod, Master of Merton College, Oxford (where Eliot resided for a few terms) comments, *Genius Loci and Other Essays* (Oxford, 1950), p. 89: "But the first of our Merton poets I remembered; and however second-rate he be, certainly he has a claim to be remembered. In the renaissance of English poetry Nicholas Grimald is, in truth, a notable name. Recalling him, I ventured to suggest that the history of English poetry might be conceived—though with some degree of paradox— as beginning with a Merton man and ending with one. It begins with Nicholas Grimald. He edited Tottel's *Miscellany*. He wrote *The Garden*. He was sentenced to be hanged, drawn, and quartered. It ends—or does it only begin again?—with Mr. T. S. Eliot. Mr. Eliot edited *The Criterion*. He wrote *The Waste Land*. He has recently been decorated with the Order of Merit. Neither of these names is negligible in the history of our poetry. If either of them seemed so to any of my audience, I could suggest, I thought, some comfort. It was a kind of comfort, however cold, to remember how bad the poets were. Nor would it be right to forget Merton poets more modern even than Mr. Eliot; to some of whom, I am told, Mr. Eliot appears already out of date."